ON DOUBT

A Univocal Book
Drew Burk, Consulting Editor

Univocal Publishing was founded by Jason Wagner and Drew Burk as an independent publishing house specializing in artisanal editions and translations of texts spanning the areas of cultural theory, media archeology, continental philosophy, aesthetics, anthropology, and more. In May 2017, Univocal ceased operations as an independent publishing house and became a series with its publishing partner the University of Minnesota Press.

Univocal authors include:

Miguel Abensour
Judith Balso
Jean Baudrillard
Philippe Beck
Simon Critchley
Fernand Deligny
Jacques Derrida
Vinciane Despret
Georges Didi-Huberman
Jean Epstein
Vilém Flusser
Barbara Glowczewski
Évelyne Grossman
Félix Guattari
David Lapoujade
François Laruelle
David Link
Sylvère Lotringer

Jean Malaurie
Michael Marder
Serge Margel
Quentin Meillassoux
Friedrich Nietzsche
Peter Pál Pelbart
Jacques Rancière
Lionel Ruffel
Felwine Sarr
Michel Serres
Gilbert Simondon
Étienne Souriau
Isabelle Stengers
Eugene Thacker
Antoine Volodine
Elisabeth von Samsonow
Siegfried Zielinski

ON DOUBT

Vilém Flusser

TRANSLATED BY RODRIGO MALTEZ NOVAES

FLUSSER ARCHIVE COLLECTION

EDITED BY SIEGFRIED ZIELINSKI

A Univocal Book

University of Minnesota Press
Minneapolis
London

This book has been published with support from the Brazilian Ministry of Culture / National Library Foundation.

Obra publicada com o apoio do Ministério da Cultura do Brasil / Fundação Biblioteca Nacional.

 MINISTÉRIO DA CULTURA
Fundação BIBLIOTECA NACIONAL

Da dúvida, 1996 © Copyright Miguel Gustavo Flusser

Originally published by Univocal Publishing, 2014.

First University of Minnesota Press edition 2021.

Copyright 2014 by the Regents of the University of Minnesota

Designed by Jason Wagner

Thanks to Edith Flusser, Dinah Flusser, Miguel Gustavo Flusser, the Vilém Flusser Archive at the Universität der Künste Berlin, Daniel Irrgang, and Jon Thrower.

Published by the University of Minnesota Press
111 Third Avenue South, Suite 290
Minneapolis, MN 55401-2520
http://www.upress.umn.edu

ISBN 978-1-5179-1293-2

A Cataloging-in-Publication record for this book is available from the Library of Congress.

Printed in the United States of America on acid-free paper

The University of Minnesota is an equal-opportunity educator and employer.

28 27 26 25 24 23 22 21   10 9 8 7 6 5 4 3 2 1

Table of Contents

FLUSSER ARCHIVE COLLECTION

Vilém Flusser is one of the most influential thinkers of media and cultural theory as well as the philosophy of communication in the second half of the twentieth century. But unlike certain thinkers of media culture such as Marshall McLuhan or Jean Baudrillard, most of his work has yet to attain the proper attention of the reading public inside and outside the walls of the academy. One of the reasons for this is due to the singular process by which Flusser constructed his thinking and writing. He is a rare polyglot who would write his texts in various languages until he was satisfied with the outcome. Fluent in Czech, German, French, English, and Portuguese, he has left an archive full of thousands of manuscripts in various languages. The Flusser Archive Collection will be a monumental step forward in finally providing an Anglophone readership with a collection of some of Flusser's most important works.

FOREWORD

Vilém Flusser wrote *Da dúvida* (*On Doubt*) in the mid-six-
ties. However, as Gustavo Bernardo pointed out, one can
find traces of its first conception in letters from the late
1950s and early 1960s.[1] This text is one of Flusser's major
early Brazilian works, alongside *Língua e realidade*[2] (*Language and Reality*) and *The History of the Devil*.[3] However,
it was not published in its original Portuguese version,
under the title *A dúvida* (*Doubt*), until 1999 by Relume
Dumará in Rio de Janeiro, eight years after Flusser's death
and more than thirty years after it was written. In 2011,
Annablume published a second edition of this version
with a new foreword by Gustavo Bernardo.[4]

In the preface to the 1999 edition, Celso Lafer mentions that in 1965 when he was a student at Cornell University he gave a German version of *A dúvida* to Hannah
Arendt at Flusser's request. Lafer mentions that he had the
opportunity to look at the text with Arendt and discuss its

1. Gustavo Bernardo, *A dúvida de Flusser. Filosofia e Literatura*, São
Paulo: Editora Globo, 2002, p. 276.

2. Vilém Flusser, *Lingua e Realidade*, São Paulo: Herder, 1963.

3. Vilém Flusser, *The History of the Devil*, Minneapolis: Univocal Publishing, 2014.

4. Vilém Flusser, *A dúvida*, São Paulo: Annablume, 2011.

contents.[5] However, since Edith Flusser intimately knew the work of her husband, and worked for years on the German translation of this text,[6] one may safely assume that Lafer's statement is probably based on a mistake. It would seem that Arendt did not truly look at the more expanded version of the text. More than likely, Lafer was referring to a shorter Portuguese version of the text, which Flusser may have translated into German specifically for Arendt. This German version has been lost.

.The shorter version in question – *Da dúvida* – was published twice: once in 1965 for the *Revista do Departamento de Humanidades* of the ITA[7] and later in 1967 as chapter five of the collection of essays *Da Religiosidade* (*On Religiosity*),[8] which was reedited in 2002.[9] In the introduction, Flusser writes that the text represents an attempt to formulate a new sense of reality by taking language as a starting point. As with the longer version, this shorter text consists of five sections. The last section, however, bears a different title. Instead of *Do sacrifício* (On Sacrifice) Flusser simply called it *Conclusão* (Conclusion). In this

5. "Eu mesmo entreguei uma versão, em alemão, de *A dúvida*, a Hannah Arendt em 1965, quando fui seu aluno em Cornell, nos EUA, a pedido de Flusser. Ela leu e comentou comigo, que o tinha achado interessante [...]." (Vilém Flusser, *A dúvida*, Rio de Janeiro: Relume Dumará, 1999, p. 12).

6. Vilém Flusser, *Vom Zweifel,* Edition Flusser, Göttingen: European Photography, 2006.

7. Volume 1, p. 7-20.

8. Vilém Flusser, *Da religiosidade*, São Paulo: Conselho Estadual de Cultura, 1967.

9. Vilém Flusser, *Da religiosidade. A literatura e o senso de realidade*, São Paulo: Escrituras, 2002, p. 47-61.

section, he refers to the crisis of Western culture and the necessity for creating a new language whose roots reach deep into the past, without mentioning the main idea of the chapter: sacrifice. This probably means that he wrote this specific chapter of *Da dúvida* only after he had written the shorter version.

Besides these two versions, there is also a third text to be considered that remains unpublished, a series of sixteen lectures delivered at the Brazilian Institute of Philosophy in São Paulo during the second semester of 1963 titled "Da dúvida e do absurdo" ("On Doubt and the Absurd").[10] In an introduction Flusser wrote in February 1965, he points out that these lectures were not originally delivered with the intention of writing a book. It was a philosophy *in fieri* that was to a great extent the result of teamwork with the students. His intention was not to convince, but to create doubt. The lecture cycle, which Flusser defines as an intellectual laboratory, was divided into two parts of eight lectures each. Among other subjects, Flusser discusses his philosophy of language, the importance of multilingualism and translation, death and immortality, as well as meditation and the play with words. Even if doubt is one of the central notions there is no single lecture dedicated to it.

Flusser most likely started out with a series of lectures in 1963, then moved on to a shorter preparatory version – around 1964/5 – and ended by writing a full-length book, probably in 1966.[11] This specific writing

10. This typescript can be examined at the Vilém Flusser Archive in Berlin.
11. According to a short editorial note in the German translation

strategy is not unusual for Flusser who often began a book by writing a series of loosely linked essays, which were collected in the end to form a single book.

At the Vilém Flusser Archive in Berlin, there are two identical typescripts of the first version of Flusser's *Da dúvida* – one of them is a carbon copy. The present English translation is based on the copy Flusser himself corrected and annotated. The front page is entirely written by hand. It contains the title of the book and the titles of each chapter along with the page numbers. At the bottom, Flusser added the last line from John Milton's poem *On His Blindness* that, because of its specific positioning, was added to the present edition as an epigraph.[12] In his early books Flusser often used quotations as epigraphs, sometimes without indicating their origin, for instance in *Das Zwanzigste Jahrhundert*[13] he used a quote from Ovid's *Tristia: Ex Ponto*. In the typescript of *Da dúvida* there are a few corrections and some sentences have been underlined. To retain this annotation they have been consequently italicized.

(Vilém Flusser, *Vom Zweifel*, Edition Flusser, Göttingen: European Photography, 2006, p. 2) and the commented biography of the still unpublished *Flusser-Quellen* (Klaus Sander, *Flusser-Quellen. Eine kommentierte Bibliographie von Vilém Flusser von 1960-2000*, p. 14), Flusser wrote the text in 1964/65. This is most likely wrong as it does not fit the timeline that can be reconstructed from the different available versions of the text and their relationship to each other.

12. The same quote can also be found at the bottom of page 99 of the present edition. In both cases, Flusser did not add any indication as to its author or source. In his Petrarchan sonnet, a poem of 14 lines, Milton discusses the Biblical parable of the talents. If one serves God to the best of one's abilities, one will meet with his approval, even when crippled or disabled.

13. Unpublished German manuscript; Vilém Flusser Archive collection.

The present edition intends to be as faithful as possible to the original text. This new English translation has succeeded in carefully reproducing Flusser's intention and captures the spirit of the original, making it one of the few major texts by Flusser to finally be available to a wider international readership. The translation is not only accurate as far as wording and sentence rhythm are concerned, but it also shows great consideration and delicacy when it comes to a proper understanding of Flusser's frequent word games, as well as his playful use of more than one language.

Rainer Guldin
Lugano, September 2014

ON DOUBT

They also serve, who only stand and wait.

John Milton, 1652.

INTRODUCTION

Doubt is a polyvalent state of mind. It could mean the end of a faith or the beginning of another. It could even, if taken to the extreme, be instituted as "skepticism," that is, as a kind of inverted faith. In moderate doses it stimulates thought. In excessive doses, it paralyzes all mental activity. Doubt, as an intellectual exercise, provides one of the few pure pleasures we know. As a moral experience, it is torture. Doubt, allied to curiosity, is the cradle of research, therefore, of all systematic knowledge. In a distilled state, doubt kills all curiosity and is the end of all knowledge.

Faith is always the starting point of doubt. Faith ("certainty") is the state of mind before doubt. Effectively, faith is the primordial state of mind. The "naive" and "innocent" spirit believes. It has "good faith." Doubt puts an end to the naivety and innocence of the spirit, and although it may produce a new and better faith, this new faith will no longer be "good." The naivety and innocence of the spirit dissolve in the corrosive acid of doubt. The climate of authenticity is irrevocably lost. The process is irreversible. Attempts to regain authenticity (original faith) by spirits that have been corroded by doubt are nothing but frustrated nostalgia. These are attempts to regain paradise. Once doubted, original "certainties" can no longer be authentically certain. Methodically applied doubt may possibly produce new, more refined and sophisticated certainties, but these will never be authentic. They will always conserve the sign of the doubt that was their midwife.

Doubt may be, therefore, conceived as a search for certainty that starts by destroying authentic certainty in order to produce an inauthentic certainty. Doubt is absurd. Therefore, the question arises: "Why do I doubt?" This question is more fundamental than the other: "Of what do I doubt?" Effectively, this is the last step of the Cartesian method, in other words: it is to doubt *doubt*. Furthermore, it is to doubt the authenticity of doubt itself. The question "why do I doubt?" implies another: "do I really doubt?"

Descartes, along with the entirety of modern thought, does not appear to go all the way to this last step. He accepts doubt as indubitable. The last Cartesian certainty, incorruptible by doubt, is: "I think, therefore, I am." It may be reformulated: "I doubt, therefore, I am." The Cartesian certainty is therefore authentic, in the sense of being naive and innocent. It is an authentic faith in doubt. This faith characterizes the entire Modern Age, whose final moments we are witnessing. This faith is responsible for the scientific and desperately optimistic character of the Modern Age, and for its unfinished skepticism, toward which we must take the last step. In the Modern Age, this faith in doubt plays the role which, during the Middle Ages, was played by the faith in God.

The doubt of doubt is a fleeting state of mind. Although it can be experienced, it cannot be sustained. It is its own negation. It vibrates, indecisively, between, on the one extreme: "everything may be doubted, including doubt itself," and on the other: "nothing can be authentically doubted." By aiming at the overcoming of the absurdity of doubt, this state of mind elevates this absurdity to the power of two. Oscillating, as it does, between radical skepticism (which it doubts) and an extremely radical, naive positivism (which it equally doubts), it does not allow the spirit a foundation to hold on to.

Kant stated that skepticism is a place of rest for reason, although it is not a dwelling. The same may be said in relation to naive positivism. The doubt of doubt does not allow for this rest. The spirit possessed by the quintessence of doubt is, in its fundamental indecision, within a situation of coming and going, which was only vaguely illustrated by the analysis of Sisyphus made by Camus. In his absurd running around, the Camusian Sisyphus is frustrated by the very thing within which he runs. Hence the basic Camusian problem: "why do I not kill myself?" The spirit possessed by the doubt of doubt frustrates itself. Suicide would not resolve its situation, since it does not sufficiently doubt the dubiousness of eternal life. Camus still nurtures a faith in doubt, although this faith is at risk within him.

"I think, therefore, I am." I think: I am a chain of thoughts. One thought follows another, therefore, I am. Why does one thought follow another? Because the first thought is not enough in itself, it demands another. It demands another in order to assure itself of itself. One thought follows another because the second doubts the first and because the first doubts itself. One thought follows another through the path of doubt. I am a chain of thoughts that doubt. I doubt. I doubt, therefore, I am. I doubt that I doubt, therefore I confirm that I am. I doubt that I doubt, therefore, I doubt that I am. I doubt that I doubt, therefore, I am, independent of any doubting. This is how, approximately, the last step of the Cartesian doubt is configured. We are at a dead-end. Effectively, we are in the cul-de-sac the Ancients reserved for Sisyphus.

The same situation may be characterized by another chain of thoughts: Why do I doubt? Because I am. I doubt, therefore, that I am. Therefore, I doubt that I doubt. It is the same cul-de-sac seen from a different angle.

This is the theoretical side of radical doubt. In fact so theoretical, that until recently, it has been dismissed, quite rightly, as a futile word game. It was an argument that could be thought, but not existentially lived (*erlebbar*). It was possible to theoretically doubt the affirmative "I am," and it was possible to theoretically doubt the affirmative "I doubt that I am," however, these doubts were nothing more than intellectual exercises that could not be translated to the level of lived experience. The few individuals who experientially lived the doubt of doubt, who authentically doubted the affirmatives "I am" and "I doubt that I am," were considered mad.

The current situation is different. The doubt of doubt spills from the intellect toward all the other layers of the mind and threatens to undermine the last pillars of our sense of reality. It is true that "sense of reality" is an ambiguous expression. It could simply mean "faith," or "mental sanity," or "the ability to choose." However, the present context proves that all three meanings are fundamentally identical. The doubt of doubt threatens to destroy the last vestiges of faith, sanity, and freedom, because it threatens to turn the concept "reality" into an empty concept, that is, impossible to be directly experienced.

The emptying of the concept "reality" accompanies the progress of doubt and is, therefore, a historical process, if seen collectively, and a psychological process, if seen individually. This is a case of progressive intellectualization. The intellect, or, that which thinks, therefore, that which doubts, invades other mental regions in order to articulate them, and makes them, for that very reason, dubious. The intellect de-authenticates all other mental regions, including those regions of the senses, which we call, in a general sense, "material reality." The doubt of doubt is the intellectualization of the intellect itself; with it, the intellect reflows over itself. It becomes dubious to itself; it de-authenticates itself. The doubt of doubt is the intellect's suicide. Cartesian doubt, as it was practiced during the Modern Age, therefore, a doubt that was incomplete, a doubt that was limited to the non-intellect accompanied by a faith in the intellect, produced a civilization and a mentality that gave refuge to reality within the intellect. Therefore, a civilization and a mentality that are "idealist." Complete doubt, the doubt of doubt, the intellectualization of the intellect, destroys this refuge and empties the concept "reality." The apparently contradictory phrases, between which the doubt of doubt oscillates, which are: "everything can be an object of doubt, including doubt itself," and "nothing can authentically be an object of doubt," are resolved at this stage of intellectual development in the phrase: "everything is nothing." Radical idealism, radical Cartesian doubt, complete intellectualization, flow into nihilism.

We are the first or second generation to have a direct experience of nihilism. We are the first or second generation of those to whom the doubt of doubt is no longer a theoretical pastime, but an existential situation. We face, in Heidegger's words, "the clear night of nothingness." In this sense we are the perfect and consequent products of the Modern Age. Through us the Modern Age achieves its aim. But the doubt of doubt, nihilism, is an unbearable existential situation. The total loss of faith, the madness of the all-enveloping nothingness, the absurdity of choice within this nothingness, are unbearable situations. In this sense, we are the overcoming of the Modern Age: through us, the Modern Age is reduced to the absurd.

The symptoms of this statement abound. The intellect's suicide, a fruit of its own intellectualization, manifests itself in every field. In the field of philosophy, it produces Existentialism and Formal Logic, two abdications of the intellect in favor of a raw and unarticulated experience, therefore, the end of philosophy. In the field of pure science, it produces manipulation through concepts that are consciously divorced from reality, which tends to transform pure science into abstract art. In the field of applied science, it consciously produces instruments destined to destroy humanity and its instruments, which are therefore, self-destructive instruments. In the field of art, it produces art that signifies itself, therefore, meaningless art. In the field of "practical reason," it produces a climate of immediate opportunism, a collective as well as individual *carpe diem,* accompanied by the emptying of all values.

Obviously, there are reactions against this progress toward nothingness. However, these reactions are reactionary, in the sense that they try to turn back the wheel of development. They are desperate. They are attempts to find reality again within the levels already vacated by the intellect in its advance. In the field of philosophy, they are characterized by the ameliorative prefix *neo* (Neo-Kantianism, Neo-Hegelianism, Neo-Thomism). In the field of pure science these reactions are characterized by the effort to reformulate the premises of scientific discipline into more modest foundations. In the field of applied science they are characterized by an already inauthentic hope of a new industrial revolution that will be capable of producing paradise on Earth. In the field of art, these reactions result in a pathetic realism called "social realism" that does not call itself "neo-realist" merely as a question of modesty. In the field of "practical reason," we see attempts to resuscitate traditional religions (sects of religions, either made up ad hoc, or sought after in geographically and historically distant regions, can be found everywhere). In the field of politics and economics, empty concepts, as well as concepts that were overcome long ago, inauthentically reemerge, as for example, the medieval concept of "sovereignty." In this field, reality is sought after, now already completely inauthentic, in the concepts of "blood" (Nazism), "class" (Marxism), or "freedom" (Neoliberalism): concepts that have been borrowed from hypothetical or semi-hypothetical past epochs. All of these reactions are condemned to failure. They want to resuscitate dead and inauthentic faiths *ab initio.*

Even though nihilism is an unbearable existential situation, it must be taken as the point of departure for every attempt at overcoming these reactions. The inauthenticity of the reactions described above resides in their ignorance (authentic or faked) of the current situation of philosophy, of pure and applied science, of art, of the individual within society, and of society before the individual; it resides in their ignorance of the fundamental problem: that in all these fields, today already highly intellectualized, doubt has dislodged faith and the sense of reality has been lost. This situation must be accepted as fact, although perhaps not as a completely consummated fact. Residues of faith can be found, as condemned remains in all fields, but more so in the field of sociology than in philosophy. We will not be able to exit the absurd situation of nihilism through them, but through nihilism itself, that is, if we exit it. In other words, this is an attempt to find a new sense of reality. This book is a modest contribution to this search within the field of philosophy.

If seen collectively, the progress of intellectualization, therefore, the progress of doubt, with its consequent emptying of the concept "reality," is a historical process. By its very nature, it manifests itself primarily in the field of philosophy, although it is silently accompanied by a parallel development in all other fields of the human situation. The advent of nihilism was, therefore, supposed and predicted by philosophers before any other field. Nietzsche frequently used the word "nihilism" in a sense similar to its meaning today. The search for a new sense of reality, in the field of philosophy, is not, therefore, something new. However, we cannot affirm that it has been accompanied, until now, by any resounding success. What emerged is a new way to philosophize, and new categories of thought.

The concept "Will" and its allied concept "experience," both of an anti-intellectual character, have been introduced. Philosophical speculation has shifted to the field of "ontology" (a prudish synonym of an ostensibly despised metaphysics), which, by itself, is a fact that proves the search for a new reality. On the other hand, studies in Logic expanded to the point where it nearly invaded the field of "ontology," which is a fact that proves philosophy's preoccupation with a new interpretation of the intellect and its function as the producer and destroyer of reality. However, as revolutionary and creative as these thoughts may be, they have not been "convincing," in the sense of generating a new sense of reality, a new "faith." On the contrary, they have contributed to the spread of nihilism, which they intended to combat, since they were intellectualizations, albeit anti-intellectual. Their decisive influence upon art and science (more specifically upon psychology) was conducive to the ultimate intellectualization of layers that, up until now, had not been invaded by the intellect. Perhaps for having been the distributors of the old reality, they contributed to the emergence of the new reality, at least negatively.

If seen individually, the progress of intellectualization, therefore the progress of doubt, is the abandonment of original faith, of "good faith," in favor of a better faith, a less naive and innocent faith. The progressive loss of the sense of reality that accompanies intellectual progress is initially experienced as liberation, a loss of prejudices, and is, therefore, an exuberant experience. However, it is accompanied from the start by an unarticulated feeling, therefore unaware of guilt. This feeling of guilt is

11

compensated in the "better faiths," which the intellect creates for itself in the course of its advance. When, at last, the intellect turns against itself, when it doubts itself, the feeling of guilt becomes conscious and articulated, and accompanied by the characteristic hesitation of supreme doubt, it dominates the scene. This climate of hesitation and guilt, or its reverse, the climate of uncommitted and unscrupulous "engagement," are therefore the symptoms of the above-mentioned philosophers. Although hesitation and the feeling of guilt are intellectually more honest than "engagement" and fanaticism, both are basically attitudes of despair. They attest to the loss of faith in the intellect, without positively contributing to an overcoming of the nihilist situation in which they find themselves. This is the scene of philosophy today.

This book does not nurture the illusion of being a great contribution to the attempt of modifying the scene. This book was born out of a loss of faith in the intellect and shall not result in any new authentic faith. However, it has the advantage of having been born later. As a consequence, it has lost the remaining naivety and innocence that still characterize the thought of its predecessors; naivety and innocence that are relative to the intellect's reach. The intellect, in other words, that which thinks and therefore doubts, has been exaggerated, also by those who have lost their faith in the intellect. Although many have recently come to understand the purely formal character of the intellect (as the Empiricists of the 17th and 18th centuries also already had), this understanding has never become part of these thinkers' authentic lived experience. Never, as I believe, has the sterility of the intellect been appreciated and grasped experientially. Never, has it been properly understood by thinkers, that is, by the intellect itself. The simple and cheap dismissal of the intellect, nurtured by sentimentalists, primitive mystics, and those who deposit all their faith in the senses, has nothing to do with the experience described here, which is the intellectual experience of the futility of the intellect. It is not, therefore, an abandonment of the intellect, but may be, on the contrary, the overcoming of the intellect by the intellect itself.

The anti-intellectualism of a large part of today's philosophy is an error and a danger. It is an error because it confuses faith in the intellect (correctly abandoned) with the framing of the intellect within a faith in a new reality to be found. It is a danger because it spreads and deepens the nihilism that it intends to combat. The intellectual experience of the sterility of the intellect, an experience that this book intends to elaborate, turns anti-intellectualism into an attitude that has been overcome. Whoever has authentically experienced, in one's intellect, the futility of the intellect, shall never be anti-intellectual again. On the contrary, this intellectual experience shall produce a positive attitude toward the intellect, now intellectually overcome. This is a situation comparable to that which emerges after a disenchantment with a large sum of money: the accumulation of the sum of money was accompanied by a faith in the saving power of money, but the possession of the money dissipated the faith. A new faith has not yet emerged to substitute the one that was lost. However, the money is still available in order to serve this new faith, if and when it is found. Anti-intellectualism is proof of the persistence of the last vestiges of faith in the intellect, and it is overcome with the disappearance of these last vestiges.

The lived experience of the intellect's sterility allows us to experience, despite not being able to comprehend, the foundations from which the intellect sprung and continues to spring: extra-intellectual foundations, which by definition, are not intellectually reachable. These may not, therefore, be authentically included in the discipline of philosophy, which is an intellectual discipline. The attempt to philosophize about these foundations is an additional error of many of today's philosophies. However, it is precisely due to their elimination from the field of philosophy, that the possibility of their inclusion into another, more appropriate field, resides. This elimination is one of the attempts of this book.

Therefore, even though the aim of this chain of thoughts cannot be the overcoming of the absurd existential situation in which we find ourselves, even though it cannot expect to overcome the nihilism into which we have fallen, it intends to shed some light upon a few aspects in order to make a future overcoming more viable. This intention alone already proves the existence of something remotely similar to faith: a hope, although faint, in the possibility of an overcoming, and therefore, in the survival of that which we very inadequately call, Western civilization. The effort of this book is dedicated to this hope.

I. On Intellect

The mental exercises that are part of the discipline of Yoga start with "concentration." Whoever is moved by curiosity or disbelief in Western methods of knowledge buys a book on the introduction to the secrets of Yoga and tries out this first mental exercise, suffers a curious shock. The book recommends, in sum, the elimination of every thought, except one, chosen arbitrarily. It seems, therefore, to be an instruction that can be easily executed. The shock resides in the incredible, ridiculous, and degrading mental gymnastics that this exercise demands. Effectively, these gymnastics are equivalent in every respect to the convulsions, repulsive to Westerns eyes, which result in the physical exercises of the yogis. Our mind contorts in this effort, just as the limbs of the yogi's body contort. We almost literally misplace our head. We generally abandon this first stage of mental exercises because it offends our aesthetic canon and our sense of dignity as intelligent people.

What is the reason for our revolt? What is the reason for our sense of inappropriateness, ridicule, and degradation that accompanies such an apparently simple exercise? It is because this exercise in concentration reveals, immediately and experientially, the struggle between Will and intellect within our mind, which intends to strengthen the Will against the intellect. Concentration is the Will's invasion of the territory of the intellect: it is the Will that eliminates all thoughts except one. This is the first step toward the conquest and destruction of the intellect by the Will; this is the aim of the discipline of Yoga. We are, however, through all of our traditions, linked to the supremacy of the intellect; we are deeply engaged in favor of the intellect in its struggle against the Will. The subordination of the Will to the intellect is, in our eyes, the "natural" state of things, therefore, the good, beautiful, and correct state. The struggle of the Will against the intellect, which seems like a revolt, represents for us, at the individual level, the struggle of madness against the forces of sanity, and at the collective level, the struggle of the "vertical irruption of barbarism" against the civilizing forces. The victory of the Will, as unimaginable as it may be for us, would be, in our eyes, an apocalyptic happening, the victory of the forces of darkness. It would be the complete inversion of the hierarchy of our values; it would be individual dementia, and the end of civilized society.

This simple exercise in concentration puts us into immediate and experiential contact with a civilization that is different from ours and with a different hierarchy of values. The exercise in concentration is not a barbaric and undisciplined act. On the contrary, it is the well-organized procedure of a refined technique, and with a pragmatically verifiable success. It has all the characteristics of being part of a civilization similar to ours. However, of a civilization that is engaged in favor of forces that seem barbaric to our eyes. It pulses for the victory of the Will over the intellect. Hence our shock; hence our revolt.

16

To be sure: our shock and our revolt are existential, not speculative. Speculatively, we have been, for a long time, accustomed to approach the struggle between the intellect and the Will with equanimity. Romanticism already exalts the Will in detriment of the intellect. Schopenhauer, who was definitely influenced by Indian society (although I doubt that he ever had the existential shock of the concentration of Yoga), concedes, in his speculations, a primordial ontological role to the Will. The whole chain of philosophical speculation from the nineteenth and twentieth centuries (perhaps the most characteristic chain) deserts the Western front in order to join the forces of the Will. However, there is something artificial and inauthentic in all of these phenomena. These are intellectual efforts to abandon the intellect, but all of these efforts lack the will to join the Will. From the existential perspective, a single effort of concentration through the rules of Yoga is worth a thousand treatises by Nietzsche or Bergson. It illuminates, in a flash of immediate experience, that which Nietzsche and Bergson intended (*inter alia*), perhaps without knowing it.

The exercise in concentration reveals, in an almost palpable manner, some aspects of the intellect and the Will, precisely for being so contrary to the "normal" (that is, traditional) workings of our mind. (I warn, casually, that I need to appeal to an allegory in order to describe a situation that goes beyond the intellect.) The situation is this: at the center there is a Self. This Self is made manifest in two ways: it *thinks* and *wants*. When concentration starts, the Self *thinks* a multiplicity of thoughts, and all of them run like threads in a loom. At the center runs the master thread, strongly lit by the attention (apparently irradiated

17

from the Self). Auxiliary threads run around the master thread, sometimes accompanying, sometimes crossing, and sometimes supporting the master thread. These auxiliary threads come from the darkness beyond the bright cone of attention. They pass, fleetingly, through the penumbra of the cone's periphery to then lose themselves in the darkness again. They are, however, always present, because the cone of attention may divert itself from the master thread to shed light upon them, thus turning them into new master threads. Simultaneously, and in a manner of speaking, on the other side, the Self *wants*; in sum: it wants to stop the master thread and thus destroy all auxiliary threads. In other words, the Self wants to think a single thought. At the end of the exercise in concentration, if it is successful, the situation will have radically changed. The Self continues at the center, and has, in front of it, a single thought, rigid, still, and dead. It would then be incorrect to say that this Self thinks. The thought that the Self has now is dead. Around this dead thought is the Self's Will, now completely free, but anchored within the dead thought. The sensation is that of an almost unlimited willpower that has no objective. This willpower starts to spin around the dead thought, spinning the dead thought in the process. Thus, a process similar to thinking emerges, however, governed by the Will and not the intellect. The Self *meditates*.

This description of the situation is satisfactory for whoever has had the direct experience of concentration and incipient meditation. It transmits in words, that is, it intellectualizes a situation that is strictly inarticulable, because it cannot be intellectualized. The words of the description are not symbolic, as in a strictly intellectual discourse, but allegorical. They do not signify, but evoke the described situation. Thanks to this evocation, they enable the intellect to penetrate the situation; they make it intelligible. However, the description is full of problems for anyone who has never had this experience, and therefore is deeply unsatisfactory. Not having been through the unarticulated, raw experience, one has to take the words of the description as univocal symbols of exact meaning. From this person's perspective – one is forced to admit – this effort to intellectualize an unarticulated situation has to be considered as a failure. This consideration reveals how the intellect is imprisoned within itself.

The description is intellectually unsatisfactory because as with every allegory, it falls into anthropomorphism. We have, in our situation, three characters, in a manner of speaking, three gods: the "Self," the "Intellect," and the "Will." We are, therefore, dangerously close to mythology. It is true that science cannot do away with these allegorical personifications by itself, and concepts such as "the Law," "Heredity," and "Consumer" prove it. However, it is no less true that demythologization continues to be an ideal of the intellectual discipline. We must, therefore, strictly speaking, confess that our situation is intellectually impenetrable and inarticulable.

This does not prevent certain aspects of this situation from becoming articulable. Although we cannot say anything intellectually satisfactory in relation to the allegorical characters of the "Self" and the "Will," having therefore to exclude them from the territory of the discussion, the same does not apply to the "Intellect." It is entirely

19

possible to demythologize the intellect. Effectively, it has not been so much personified in the allegory as much as it has been "thingified," by being compared with a loom whose threads are thoughts. It is only necessary to let go of the image of the loom and the threads; it is only necessary to dematerialize the image, and the allegory disappears. Then the description of the intellect becomes symbolic, that is, it acquires an exact meaning. This is the description: *the intellect is the field within which thoughts occur.* The purist may object that the concept "field" is also allegorical. However, this is a concept employed at another level of meaning by the exact sciences. But since we do not have to be realists, we shall keep our description of the intellect as the operative hypothesis.

If we describe the intellect as a field within which thoughts occur, we overtake the Cartesian affirmative "I think therefore I am" by at least one step; we push the Cartesian doubt one step further. Our description of the intellect allows us to doubt the affirmative "I think," and to substitute it by the affirmative "thoughts occur." The affirmative "I think" is an abbreviation of the affirmative "there is a Self that thinks." The Cartesian method only proves the existence of thoughts, never the existence of a Self that thinks. It does not allow the affirmative "I think." The affirmative "I think therefore I am" is an abbreviation of the affirmative "there is a Self that thinks, therefore there is a Self that exists." This is a pleonastic affirmative, as well as naturally dubious.

The intellect, described as a field in which thoughts occur, is simultaneously a more restricted and broader concept than the dubious concept of Self. It is a more restricted concept because the Self (whatever its reality may be; now already very empty due to our doubt) does not exhaust itself by thinking. For example: the Self also has *wants*. The intellect is a wider concept because the Self does not encompass the whole field in which thoughts occur. Even if we were to extend the parameters of the concept of the Self, to include all of the individual Selves in it (as some of today's psychologists do), this super-dubious Super-Self still would not encompass the whole field in which thoughts occur. For example, thoughts that are mechanically produced by electronic instruments also occur. The Self, being simultaneously a more restricted and broader concept than the intellect, is a dispensable concept when we consider the intellect. It must be eliminated from the discussion about the intellect, not only because of its dubiousness and the reasons exposed during the discussion about concentration, but also by the principle of the economy of concepts, by the concept of *Occam's razor*. However, this elimination is an ideal that is difficult to realize at the current developmental stage of philosophical discussion. We are all, including this book, too imprisoned within the concept of Self in order to be able to authentically abandon it. However, the liberation from the Self is no longer an objective reserved for mystics, as it was not so long ago: it is reachable through intellectual speculation, as the present argument demonstrates.

The intellect, described as a field in which thoughts occur, dispenses with the question: "What is the intellect?" A field is not a *what*, but the way *how* something occurs. The gravitational field of the Earth is not a thing, but *how* the bodies related to the Earth behave. In the same manner, the intellect is how thoughts behave, the structure within which and according to which thoughts occur. The intellect has no ontological dignity without thoughts; it is not a Being as such. Inversely, there are no thoughts without the intellect. In order to occur, thoughts must occur somehow, and this *how* is the intellect. In sum: the question "what is the intellect?" lacks meaning. It is a naive and metaphysical question, in the pejorative sense of the word, just like questions such as "what is beauty?" and "what is goodness?" Intellectuals and anti-intellectuals are both prisoners of this type of naive metaphysics. The question that imposes itself is the following: "what is a thought?" Our comprehension or lack of comprehension of the concept "intellect" will depend upon the answer to this question; therefore we must dedicate our attention toward this question in what follows.

In order to do so, let us return to the consideration of the Yoga exercise in concentration. If we contemplate that which we call "thought" from our "natural," "normal," that is, traditionally Western perspective, then thought is seen as a psychological phenomenon, as something that is intimately and immediately given. However, if we contemplate thought within the exercise of concentration, it presents itself as an external phenomenon, as something among the things that make up the environment called "world." From this perspective, thoughts are seen as a dense and opaque web that obstructs our vision of reality, but through which the light of this reality infiltrates, refracted and strained. The web of thoughts seems like a layer that interposes itself between the "Self" and reality, covering the view of reality, indirectly presenting this reality to the "Self," and then representing this reality to the "Self." The words "cover," "present" and "represent," are homonymic in German as, *vorstellen*. The web of thoughts is that which Schopenhauer calls *Vorstellung*, which he contrasts with the "Will." Therefore, according to Hindu teachings, the web of thoughts is the veil woven by illusions that must be torn, which they call *Māyā*.

This perspective on thought, let us say an inside-out perspective, provides the possibility of an "objective" appreciation, because within it, thought is seen as the object and not the subject, of contemplation. Thus it becomes a phenomenon in the Husserlian, phenomenological sense, that is, it becomes something to be understood. We may, from this point onward, direct ourselves against thought and investigate it. Firstly, we shall discover that thought, far from being a simple phenomenon, is a complex of elements, organized among themselves according to fixed rules. We call these elements "concepts" and the rules "logic": thought is a logical organization of concepts.

Secondly, we shall discover that thought is a process, which can be thought of in two senses. In the first sense, thought is a process that runs in search of its own completion. We may conceive of interrupted, and therefore incomplete, thoughts. Thought is a process in search of form (*Gestalt*); it is an aesthetic process. Once this form is achieved, the thought acquires an experiential aura of satisfaction, the climate of a complete and perfect work of art. This aura is called "meaning." A complete thought is meaningful. In the second sense, thought is a self-reproductive process; a new thought is automatically

23

generated. We may distinguish chains of thought within which individual thoughts form links; these chains are connected to each other as if by hooks in order to form the fabric of thought, within which the chains of thoughts are the threads. An individual thought, although aesthetically complete for being meaningful, is however, charged with an internal dynamism that prevents it from resting alone. This inherent dynamism within thought manifests itself through a tendency for the thought to overcome itself, abandoning itself through this overcoming. This abandonment of thought through itself may assume several forms, but the one that leads to the formation of new thoughts, therefore the only one that matters in the present context, is also called "logic." Logic is, therefore, an ambivalent concept. It is the set of rules according to which thought completes itself, as well as the set of rules according to which thought multiplies.

The web of thoughts may be conceived as a dynamic set of organizations of concepts, which hides and reveals reality, or, which introduces the Self to reality in a *distorted* manner through its own rules, or, which presents reality to the Self distorted through the rules of thought. Reality presents itself to thought as it does, because that is how the web of thoughts is constructed. The web of thoughts cannot grasp "Reality in itself," because this web only obeys the rules that are inherent to the web itself. In this conception, the web of thoughts corresponds to Kant's "pure reason," and the rules to his "categories of pure reason." This conception is the one we are accustomed to through classic philosophical discussion; even though it may seem to be a critical conception of thought and even though it may seem to admit the limitations of the intellect, it operates, nonetheless, with the concept of knowledge as *adequatio intellectus ad rem*; an adequation which it negates in its premises. It admits, moved by a naive faith in the intellect, that reality in itself shines through the web of thoughts, albeit *distorted*; although it simultaneously admits the impossibility of any affirmative in relation to reality in itself. This is a conception that must be abandoned.

By abandoning this classic conception we shall have, possibly, the first vision of the force that propels the web of thoughts. This web may be conceived as being a single enormous super-thought in search of its completion. As it presents itself to us now, incomplete and interrupted by our contemplation, it has no meaning, in the same way incomplete and interrupted thoughts have no meaning. The force that propels the web of thought is the search for meaning, and it is this search that presents itself as being absurd, frustrated by the very character of thought. In this conception, the meanings of individual thoughts acquire a secondary and parasitic role. Individual thoughts are meaningful as long as they contribute to a general meaning, and the web of thoughts expands in search of such meaning. The fact that they are meaningful in this way contributes to the expansion of the web. The sum of the meaning of individual thoughts is the web's power of expansion. However, since this ultimate meaning, toward which thoughts tend, is unreachable, the meanings of individual thoughts are then, in this sense, also meaningless. Nevertheless, they continue to be meaningful within their contexts. The abandonment of faith in the ultimate meaning of thought does not necessarily lead to the abandonment of the pragmatic use of the meaning of individual thoughts. In this abandonment of the practical use, in this reaction of "all or nothing," resides the error and the primitivism of anti-intellectualists.

Let us reformulate our conception of the web of thoughts in light of the preceding considerations. It is a dynamic set of organizations of concepts that absconds reality in the effort to ultimately reveal it: it is a search for reality that starts by abandoning it. It is an absurd effort. The web of thoughts is, therefore, identical to doubt, as we have discussed it in the introduction of this book. If we described the intellect as the field within which thoughts occur, that is, as the field within which the web of thoughts is in expansion, we may now condense our description by saying: *the intellect is the field of doubt.*

II. On Phrase

The point of view asserted in the last chapter reveals, in a manner of speaking, the anatomy and the physiology of thought. It reveals thought as an organization of concepts and reveals the workings of thought.

Let us consider thought as an organization of concepts. Therefore, our investigation leads us to the next question: "what is a concept?" Although it is the element of thought, we do not dispose of a clear and univocal definition of the concept "concept." This circumstance reveals the unconfessed faith of our thinkers upon the intellect. This faith commands the concept to be something that accompanies (or that should accompany) the word. The naive student in *Faust* says: "*Doch ein Begriff muss bei dem Worte sein*" ("However, a concept must accompany a word"). Goethe shares the student's naivety and distinguishes words that are, and words that are not, accompanied by concepts. He finds himself in excellent company. Every effort to define "concept" is an attempt to paraphrase the following article of faith: "Concept is the unarticulated foundation from which a legitimate word emerges." On the other hand, concept is not *something*, but *of something*; to speak plainly, concept is a trace that a "thing" leaves in the intellect. We are, therefore, facing a curious situation. In the first conception the word is the symbol of the concept. In the second conception the concept is the symbol of something. Concept is therefore something between word and thing – something completely superfluous, effectively, introduced only in the effort to overcome the abyss between word and thing. There are no concepts without words, and to say that there are words without concepts is nothing but a superficial way of speaking. What this suggests is that there are words without a corresponding "thing" (whatever the meaning of such a metaphysical statement may be). Therefore, strictly speaking, there are no words without concepts. That is, there are incomprehensible words. These are not legitimate words, in the sense that they are not part of a meaningful phrase – but this is a problem that will come later. It is enough, for now, to affirm that there are no words without concepts or concepts without words, and that consequently "concept" and "word" are synonyms in the logical sense. They differ emotionally, with the role of conciliation between faith and intellect being ascribed to "concept," but logically they coincide. We can, therefore, as a matter of economy, let go of the use of the word "concept" in favor of the word "word." Thought is, therefore, an organization of words.

With this reformulation, we have shifted every consideration of thought, and with it every consideration of intellect, onto a completely different terrain – effectively, onto an adequate terrain. What before could have been interpreted as a psychological exercise or metaphysical speculation, now acquires its exact place within the body of research disciplines: the preoccupation with thought, the consideration of the intellect, is part of the discipline of language. If the element of thought is the word, then thought becomes a linguistic organization, and the intellect becomes the field in which linguistic organizations occur. If we describe thought as a process, we can, as of now, specify what type of process it is: it is the articulation of words. This articulation does not need organs or instruments in order to be processed; organs and instruments may be employed *a posteriori* in order to produce this secondary articulation that is spoken or written language. Primary articulation, unexpressed language, "whispering," is identical to the web of thoughts. These rules, according to which thoughts formulate themselves and multiply, are the rules of language. "Logic" and "grammar" become synonyms in the same way that "concept" and "word" are. If we define "language" as "the field in which word organizations occur," "language" becomes synonymous with the "intellect" and the study of the intellect, or the study of the language that the intellect is, becomes a rigorous discipline.

At this point in the argument, it is necessary to make a salvo. Linguistic studies, as we presently know them, cannot distinguish between primary and secondary language, between pure language and expressed, applied language. As a consequence, the pure, formal and structural aspects of language become mixed with the aspects that are proper to applied language. For example, words are sometimes considered as symbols (pure aspect) and at other times as a group of phonemes (applied aspect). The history of the word is sometimes considered as the body of its modifications in relation to meaning (pure aspect), and at other times as the body of its modifications in relation to its sensible form (applied aspect). There are attempts to discover laws, according to which grammatical rules develop (pure aspect), and there are attempts to discover laws according to which new types of words develop (applied aspect). As a consequence, a fundamental confusion within recent linguistic studies reigns.

Although it is not always easy to distinguish between pure and applied language, because of the intimate relation that exists between them, this distinction is always possible. It needs to be done, and the study of language needs to be divided according to it. The part that occupies itself with applied language needs to be relegated to the field of the natural sciences, and it will have little or nothing to do with the problems of thought. The other part will form what Dilthey referred to as "science of the spirit" (*Geisteswissenschaft*), with the only difference being that it shall be a de-psychologized science. This science shall be just as exact, or not so exact, as the natural sciences are. This science of pure language is, for now, only *in statu nascendi*. The work of formal logicians such as Carnap and Wittgenstein, and the verbal experiences of existentialists such as Heidegger and Sartre, are nothing more than approximations of the institution of such a science. We must continue, therefore, with our investigation of thought without the decisive support of this discipline yet to be established.

We defined thought as an organization of words. The linguistic sciences call organizations of words "phrases." "Thought" and "phrase" are, therefore, synonyms just like "concept" and "word" are. *The intellect is the field in which phrases occur*. The analysis of the phrase and of the relation between phrases is equivalent to the analysis of the intellect. Let us sketch an analysis of the phrase: generally speaking, we can distinguish five organs within a standard phrase: (1) subject, (2) object, (3) predicate, (4) attribute, and (5) adverb. 4 and 5 are complements of 1, and respectively, 2 is of 3. We can say that, basically, the standard phrase consists of subject, object, and predicate. The subject is the group of words within the phrase, about which the phrase is going to speak. The object is the group of words toward which the phrase is directed. The predicate is the group of words that unites the subject and object. This description of the phrase is, without a doubt, an excessive simplification of the situation. There are enormously complex phrases that consist of interlinked phrases and sub-phrases, with a wealth of complements and additives that are difficult to analyze. And there are defective phrases, in which a subject, object, and predicate are apparently missing. However, even so, by simplifying the standard phrase, its analysis shall reveal the fundamental aspects of the process called "thought."

Thus, the phrase has two horizons: subject and object. It is a process that is projected from one horizon toward the other. To be more precise: something projects itself in the phrase from one horizon, which is the subject, toward the other, which is the object, and this something is the predicate. The phrase is a project, within which the projectile (the predicate) projects itself from the subject in demand of an object. Subject and object, as horizons of the project, do not properly participate in its dynamic. They are the static parts of the project. The predicate, the missive, or *missile,* which projects itself along the trajectory that links a subject and an object in order to form the project, is the real message of the phrase. That is where we must look for the meaning of the phrase. Given the importance of the analysis of the phrase for the comprehension of the intellect, it will be necessary to consider each of its organs a little closer.

Let us first consider the implications of having defined the phrase as being a project. This shall ease the comprehension of the function of the organs within the phrase's organism. The word "project" is a concept with which Existential philosophy operates (*Entwurf*); according to this school of thought we are here (we exist), because we were thrown (*geworfen*) here. Two situations may result from having been thrown here: we may continue to passively fall into the world of things, which envelops and oppresses us; falling toward death, or we may turn against our origins, from which we were thrown, thus transforming the things that envelop us into instruments that attest to our passage through them – we may project ourselves. The first situation, that of decadence, the Existentialists call inauthentic; the second situation, that of the project, they call authentic. The discussion of the merits of this view of existence is not appropriate here. What is appropriate here is the consideration that, having defined the phrase (that is, thought) as a project, we have framed the concept "thought" within this view. Effectively, not only have we framed thought within the Existentialist vision, but we have also liberated Existentialism from the opprobrium of the anti-intellectualism that hovers above it. Thought (the phrase), is not simply *one* among the projects through which we project ourselves against

32

being thrown here; thought *is,* effectively, our master project, the standard according to which all other secondary projects are realized. Thought is a project because it is the way through which existence projects itself against its origins. Here we see, under another prism, the aspect of absurdity, of anti-faith, of the doubt that is thought. However, the word "project" acquires, within this context, a quality that it does not have within Existentialist discussions. It becomes analyzable. For the Existentialists, the project is an experience accompanied by a climate (*Stimmung*). Within the present context it continues to be an experience (we all have it by having thoughts), and it is, nonetheless, accessible to analysis. Let us proceed with this analysis.

The subject, the starting point of the project that is the phrase, is considered, on its own, as detritus of a previous phrase. It is what remains of a thought already perfected and realized. It is the link that unites the phrase, yet to be projected, to the phrase that immediately or medially anteceded it. Even though the project may have been predicated as the subject in a previous phrase, or even though it may have been reached as the object of a previous phrase, the project is not exhausted. There is still something left to be predicated in relation to it, or there is still something to be reached within it: this something must be predicated within the new project that is being projected. The phrase is, therefore, a project that intends to successively predicate everything in relation to its subject, until it has been exhausted. A chain of thoughts shall be considered as being complete only if the complete exhaustion of the subject is achieved; only if everything in relation to the

33

subject has been predicated. This is an absurd effort, both practically and theoretically. The object, the aim of the project that is the phrase, is what the project invests against, and what the project searches and investigates. If the object is reached in its fullness, it will practically be swallowed by the subject, and will be able to figure as an attribute of the subject in a subsequent phrase.

The predicate, the center of the project that is the phrase, unites within it, in a dialectic synthesis, the subject's thesis to the object's antithesis, and this synthesis is precisely what the phrase is. This union between subject and object attained through the predicate is called "the meaning of the phrase." In order to be able to better comprehend the function of each one of the organs of the phrase, as it has been sketched, let us visualize the situation:

As an example, let us take the phrase: "the man washes the car." In this phrase "the man" is the subject, "the car" is the object, and "washes" is the predicate. The subject "the man" irradiates the predicate "washes" toward the object "the car." The phrase therefore has the form (*Gestalt*) of target practice: the subject ("the man") is the gun, the predicate ("washes") is the bullet, and the object ("the car") is the target. We may even visualize the situation by comparing it to a cinematographic projection: the subject ("the man") is the projector, the predicate ("washes") is the projected image, and the object ("the car") is the screen. I believe that the visualization of the form (*Gestalt*) of the phrase is of utmost importance for the comprehension of the intellect. Comparative psychologists affirm, in their attempt to explain the effective world of spiders, that their world is reduced to happenings that take place upon the threads of the web. Happenings that take place in the intervals between the threads of the web do not participate in the spider's effective (real = *wirklich*) world, but are potentialities; the spider's becoming. They are the unarticulated, chaotic, and "metaphysical" backdrops of a philosophizing spider. The philosopher-spider affirms, negates or doubts the meta-web happenings, the poet-spider intuits them, the creator-spider endeavors to precipitate everything upon the web's threads in order to comprehend and devour everything, and the mystic-spider precipitates itself into the web's intervals in order to fuse itself with the whole and become free from the limitations of the web through a mystical union. The spider is an animal that is extremely grateful to comparative psychology, because it has a visible web; the other animals, including man, must be content with invisible webs. Man's web consists of phrases; the form (*Gestalt*) of the human web is the phrase. By visualizing the web of man's effective, real, *wirklich* world, we shall be visualizing the structure of "reality."

Let us detain ourselves for a moment on the spider. What happens upon the threads of the web? Flies, other spiders, and catastrophes that tear the threads happen. And, at the center of the web there is a happening that is unreachable through the web, the spider itself – the secretor and owner of the web, free to move around the threads in order to eat flies, copulate with other spiders, fight other spiders, and fix any damage in the web caused by catastrophes. We may, therefore, basically distinguish the following ontological modalities, the following forms of Being: fly, other spider, destructive catastrophe, and, together with all of its web-problematics, the spider itself. The civilized spider, in the Western sense of the term, will tend to disregard the difference between *fly* and *other spider,* considering the other spider as a kind of fly, it will tend to explain the destructive catastrophes of the web as super-flies that the web cannot bear (provisionally, since the web grows and becomes stronger, and will eventually be able to bear flies of any size); and it will tend to consider the meta-web world as a reservoir; a becoming of flies. The materialist spider will teach that the fly is the thesis and the spider itself the antithesis of the dialectic process that occurs upon the web's threads, which will have reached the last synthesis once the spider has eaten all the flies. The Hegelian spider will affirm that the spider presupposes the fly, and that the dialectic process is a progressive arachnation of the fly-world (therefore phenomenal), and that consequently, the eating of the fly is equivalent to the realization of the fly. The eaten fly, as a realized fly, is thus the last synthesis, the total realization of flies through arachnation. The Heideggerian spider will consider the fly to be eaten as a condition (*Bedingung*) of the spider-situation, and the cadaver of the already eaten fly as a witness (*Zeug*) of the spider's passage through the fly-world. These three types of Western speculation, as well as other similar ones, are characterized by an extreme arachnism, since they accept the web as the foundation of reality without discussing the web itself. Arachnism is unavoidable for the spiders, but the discussion of the web is arachnally possible. This discussion makes viable a more appropriate vision not only of the fly, but also of the spider.

Let us return to the human web, exemplified by the phrase "the man washes the car." This situation is unarguably more complicated than the one in the spider's web. Several types of words ("flies"), that is, subject, predicate, and object, happen upon it. Nevertheless, the parallel can be maintained. Our effective, real, *wirklich* world exhausts itself through one of those many types of words. The rest is the chaotic, unarticulated world of becoming, which escapes through the weave of our web; a world that may perhaps be poetically or mystically intuited, but which is realizable only through words organized according to the rules of our web. In order to be real, everything needs to assume the form of a subject, object, or predicate within a phrase. That which Wittgenstein calls *Sachverhalt,* that is, the behavior of things among themselves, and that which Heidegger calls *Bewandtnis,* that is, the existent agreement between things, is nothing more than the relation between subject, object, and predicate. Our world of real things, that is, the web of our phrases, is organized; it is a cosmos; it is a *Sachverhalt* and it has a *Bewandtnis,* because our phrases are thus constructed. It is evident that each particular language, if it is of the fusional type, has either a slightly different or a very different type of phrase construction. Therefore, each particular language has a different *Sachverhalt* and a different *Bewandtnis*: a different cosmos. What we are discussing in the course of these considerations is, *sensu stricto,* the cosmos that corresponds to the Portuguese language. Given the structural parentage between the fusional languages, it may be applied, with certain reservations, to the whole cosmoi of fusional languages.

By attempting to visualize the form of the phrase, we are effectively attempting to visualize the cosmos of our reality; we are investigating the real *Sachverhalt* and are seeking to know what *Bewandtnis* it has. If we visualize the phrase as a target practice or a cinematographic projection, we are affectively thus visualizing our cosmos. By saying that the phrase consists of subject, object, and predicate, organized among themselves in the form of a project comparable to target practice or a projection, we are effectively saying that our reality consists of subjects, objects, and processes thus organized. The logical analysis of the phrase is an ontological analysis.

Things behave within reality just as they behave within the phrase "the man washes the car." Hence, every ontological investigation should start from the analysis of the phrase. Just as the spider must consider its web before any consideration about flies, if it wants to avoid a naive arachnism, we must consider, before anything else, the structure of the phrase, if we want to avoid the naive attitude called, nowadays, "humanism." This structure is given to us through the language within which we think, just as irrevocably as it is given to the spider through the web. To wish to escape from the structure of the reality of subject, object, and predicate, is to wish to fall into a metaphysical suicide, into the weaves of our web. A reality that consists only of subjects (Parmenidean madness), or objects (Platonic madness), or predicates (Heraclitean madness), is an example of this type of suicidal escape. As uncomfortable as it may be, we must accept the triple ontology as a given, imposed by language. The rest is metaphysics; therefore, silence.

Subject, object, and predicate are therefore the forms of Being that make up our reality. Let us consider the subject. It is the detonator of the phrase. It is not enough in itself; it needs the phrase in order to fit within reality. The subject, in our example "the man," lacks meaning if considered in isolation. It is the detritus of a preceding phrase, for example the phrase "this is a man." It is, however, charged with explosive force, and it is becoming a subject due to this charge. This explosive charge is its search for meaning. In seeking to signify, that is, in seeking a place within the structure of reality, the word "the man" becomes the subject in a phrase: it seeks a *Sachverhalt* that has a *Bewandtnis*. In other words: it seeks to be predicated toward an object. "Man," if considered in isolation, without a phrase, is a search, an interrogation, and should be written, strictly speaking, "man?" The subject, the foundation of the phrase, that which Aristotle and the Scholastics called *substantia*, is a being in search of an object in order to be realized. It lacks something against which it may be projected in a predicate.

Let us consider this something, that is, the object — in our example the word "car," as that which blocks the subject's project; it is the obstacle that ends the subject's search. The object opposes itself to the subject's search, and in this sense it endows meaning to this search. It defines the subject within a situation, within a *Sachverhalt*, which is the phrase. It limits the subject, hence endowing it with a place within the scheme of reality. It realizes the subject, but it realizes itself through the same process. If considered in isolation, without a phrase, the object is something not yet found, but which must be found. The object without a phrase is an imperative, the subject's duty, and should be written, strictly speaking, in our example, "car!" Once reached by the subject, the object's imperative fuses with the subject's interrogative within the indicative of the *Sachverhalt* that is the phrase. The project of the phrase – interrogative if seen subjectively, or imperative if seen objectively – is an indication if seen as *Sachverhalt,* that is, as a whole.

If we consider our reality from the subject's perspective, which we may call "subjectivist eccentricity," it shall present itself as a single and enormous search and interrogation, as a search for meaning. This subjectivist eccentricity characterizes, for example, Romantic thought. If we consider our reality from the object's perspective, which we may call "objectivist eccentricity," it shall present itself as a single and enormous obstacle, as a categorical barrier that determines us, and empires above us. This objectivist eccentricity, confessedly or unconfessedly, characterizes Marxist thought, for example. The apparent dichotomy between the two eccentricities dissolves in view of the whole phrase, in which both the subject and object have *Bewandtnis.* Reality presents itself, from this perspective, as an indication, that is, as an articulation, a linguistic organization that overcomes the interrogative and the imperative through the *Sachverhalt* between subject and object. The object reached by the subject in the phrase reveals the eternal quarrel between determinists and indeterminists as being a quarrel between eccentrics, or a quarrel born out of a false grammar.

The words "subject" and "object," if considered etymologically in the sense of "pure language," (as I indicated above) should not give a lot of margin for confusion. "Subject" is that which is at the base of the project (*subjectum*). "Object" is that which is opposed to the project (*ob-jectum*). However, both words have been, for thousands of years, part of the philosophical conversation and have been used outside of their authentic context, which is grammar. Thus, they have given origin to multiple metaphysical speculations that must be taken to the absurd, if these words were to be put back into their context. For example: the distinction between "real object" and "ideal object," or the identification of "subject" with "I," or with "God." Within the examples cited and others, these are simple errors of syntax. I hope this discussion will contribute to the elimination of these errors and also put both words back into their structurally correct context, that is, within the structure of fusional languages.

The opposition between subject and object within the phrase is overcome by the predicate. The predicate establishes the *Sachverhalt* between subject and object. The predicate occupies, therefore, the central position within the project that is the phrase. The word "predicate" itself demands a patient ontological investigation that goes well beyond the scope of this book. It emerged from the word "dictum" and has a close affiliation with the words "predict" (that is, prophesize) and "preach." It is a word that is intimately linked to all of the ontological problems that crowd around the words "to say," "to speak," and "language." The consideration of the predicate leads us to the core of language. Subject and object are the horizons of the phrase, thus, of language, but the predicate is the center, the essence of the phrase, therefore, of language.

Although we are condemned, by the structure of language, to the triple ontology (subject, object, and predicate), the predicate is ascribed a primordial importance. Let us consider the predicate.

In our earlier example we have the predicate "washes," which makes an effort to unite the subject and the object as a *Sachverhalt* within the phrase. That is, it makes the effort to integrate the subject and the object within the structure of reality. This is, however, an absurd effort by definition. The subject and the object cannot be integrated within the structure of reality. Let us exemplify this absurdity: "the man" is real because he "washes," therefore he is real only as long as he "washes." "The car" is real because "the man washes it," therefore it is real only as long as "the man washes it." The reality of the "man" and the "car" is in "washes." "The man" is the subjective side while "the car" is the objective side of reality, which in its turn is the predicate "washes." However, "the man" and "the car" transcend the reality that is the predicate "washes." We may verify this transcendence by establishing another *Sachverhalt* between the same subject and the same object by predicating another predicate, for example "the man drives the car." Now the same "man" and the same "car" are realized within a different reality, which is the predicate "drives." What gives us the authority to say that these two realities consist of the "same" subject and object? This is an eternal question that is typical of Classical philosophy, which has also given rise to countless metaphysics and epistemologies. However, within the present context, the answer is simple and has no mystery. It is a purely formal question and relates to the syntax of whichever language we are thinking within. We are authorized to speak of "the same" subject and of "the same" object because in both phrases the same words serve as subject and object. In summary, we may say that the subject and the object, for being able to participate in different *Sachverhalte,* transcend them all, and more: since the subject and the object can participate in countless *Sachverhalte,* they transcend countless *Sachverhalte.* Reality is a collection of *Sachverhalte,* that is, a collection of phrases. Therefore, we may say that the subject and object transcend reality while taking part in countless *Sachverhalte.* The reality of all *Sachverhalte* is in their predicate.

Classical philosophy knows the concept of "predicative thinking." It recognizes the intellect's limitation in being able to "grasp" (*erfassen*) only the predicates of a subject, but never the subject itself. However, as Classical philosophy does not frame the problem within the grammatical context, it loses itself in sterile speculations. The intellect's limitation is given by the structure of language, and in this specific case, the structure of the phrase in fusional languages. Therefore, as it is, this structure is resumed to the reality of each *Sachverhalt* in the predicate of each phrase. Strictly speaking, we may say that *reality is the sum of the predicates of every articulable phrase.*

Subject and object, the horizons of the phrase, form the links between phrases and guarantee, in this way, the continuity of reality. For example: "The man washes the car. Later, the man drives the car." These two *Sachverhalte* participate in the same *continuum* of reality because both phrases contain the same subject and the same object. By approaching the problem of reality's flux from a grammatical point of view, the eternal quarrel between Parmenides and Heraclitus is overcome. Subject and object, the immutable "*onta*" of Pre-Socratic speculation, transcend the Heraclitean river in the sense that they only participate in it in order to guarantee its flux. Strictly speaking, they are not part of the river; they are not "real" in the Pre-Socratic sense. Precisely because they are immutable, that is, not completely predicable, they are not properly "*onta*." They are the limits and the aims of the predicates.

The predicate "means" the subject and the object; within the predicate the subject and the object acquire meaning. The predicate is the subject and the object transformed into a signal, a sign. Outside the phrase, "man" and "car" are meaningless symbols precisely because they are in search of meaning, but as the subject and object of this phrase they acquire the meaning "washes." They become signs thanks to "washes." As signs they transcend the *Sachverhalt*; as symbols, and by having meaning, they participate in it. The *Sachverhalt* (the phrase) is meaningful in the sense that it transforms symbols into signs. Reality is the process that transforms symbols into signs by predicating symbols. Subject and object are reality's becoming, because they are the becoming of the phrase, within which they shall acquire meaning.

One of the most powerful Brazilian thinkers, Vicente Ferreira da Silva, advocates (if I understand him correctly) the reconquering of the symbolic vision of things. He says that rational thought puts things within a context (*Sachverhalt*) that is manipulable by the same rational thought, and thus violates them. The symbolic vision puts things back within an authentic whole, which is reality. Thus, instead of knowing and manipulating things, we only "recognize" them. What Ferreira da Silva advocates, effectively, is the abandonment of the intellect and of reality, such as it emerges through the phrases of fusional languages. He advocates a fall from the web into the chaos of the becoming of phrases that are precisely the symbols to be signified in the phrases. He advocates something unrealizable, because it is unthinkable by the intellect ruled by the structure of fusional languages. He advocates "symbolic thinking" and "to think without phrases," therefore, "to think without thinking," therefore, the impossible. Ferreira da Silva is an example of Faustian and noble attempts to obviate the linguistic process, to grasp the subject and object outside of the phrase, and to find a shortcut to reality. He is not aware of the impossibility to obviate this effort, even being conscious of the frustration of the intellectual effort, in its advance, to predicate subjects and objects. Having passed through the stage of mumbling signs such as "the man" and "the car," he shall end up flowing into a metaphysical silence.

The phrase is the only way, even though it is frustrated, through which symbols are realized because it is the only way through which they acquire meaning. It is the only way because that is how our intellect is built. And it is frustrated because the subject and the object are inexhaustible; they are not completely predicable. The intellect advances from phrase to phrase, therefore, from predicate to predicate, in the effort to exhaust the subject and the object, to fully signify the subject and the object, without ever being able to reach its aim. It advances from partial meaning to partial meaning in search of an unreach-able full meaning; thought is a single unfinished phrase, therefore, never meaningful. *Thought is a single enormous predicate emitted by a never predicable subject toward an un-reachable object.* However, thought is the only way through which the subject can acquire meaning and reach the object. Our reality as a whole resides in this advance of thought, which is the advance of language. Our reality is an unfinished and interminable phrase in search of an unreachable meaning of the subject and the object that transcend the phrase. The partial meanings of subaltern phrases, which compose our reality, are the cosmos that we have already conquered from the chaos of becoming, from the chaos of meaningless symbols. Therefore, even though the intellect is a frustrated effort, it is also a pro-ductive effort. Effectively, it is the only productive effort given to us. The sum of the partial predicates is the sum of our realizations. To be understood, within this context, "we" is a synonym of "language." The sum of the already articulated predicates is the conversation that we are, and the predicates yet to be articulated are our meaning.

The analysis of the phrase is equivalent, as has already been said, to the analysis of thought. The chosen example, "the man washes the car" is the example of an exception-ally simple phrase. Its analysis reveals only vulgar and less differentiated aspects of language; nevertheless, it reveals that which is fundamental for the comprehension of thought. Condensing what this chapter made the effort to demonstrate, we may affirm the following: The intellect is the field in which thoughts occur. Thoughts are phrases of a given fusional language. Phrases are analyzable through words with different functions. The three most important functions, the only ones that are ontologically decisive, are the subject, object, and predicate. Subject and object are the horizons of the phrase in the sense that they transcend it as symbols. However, they participate in the phrase as signs signified by the predicate. The intellect may be redefined, in the light of this analysis, as the field in which predicates signifying subjects and objects occur. The intellect is therefore the field in which the predicative search for meaning, starting from the subject that demands an object, occurs. This definition of the intellect is an explication of the definition from which this chapter started, to be sure: the intellect is the field of doubt. The character of doubt has become more explicit. It is the linguistic activity of predicating. The limitations of doubt, that is, the limitations of the intellect, have also become clearer. They are the subject and the object. Subject and object are words of a certain type. They are names. The limitations of the intellect are names. The limitations of doubt are names. The limitations of language are names. Our investigation leads, as a next step, to the consideration of names.

III. On Name

The purpose of this book is to discuss the intellect and its limitations, with the aim of contributing toward the overcoming of the current situation of our civilization. This situation was characterized, in the introduction, as a nascent nihilism, the fruit of an excessive valorization of the intellect accompanied by despair in relation to the intellect's ability to put us in touch with "reality." At the current stage of our cultural development, we are reaching the intellectualization of every layer of mental activity, including the layer of the intellect. This intellectualization of the intellect has been called, in the introduction, the "doubt of doubt." The intellect is our only avenue of access toward reality, and this avenue is blocked by the intellectualization of the intellect. Hence, our nihilism.

In order to overcome this super-valorization of the intellect and this despair in relation to the intellect, we have resolved to attempt to analyze it; instead of abandoning it, as so many do nowadays. This analysis, as rough as it may have been, has revealed the frontiers of the intellect. These frontiers are not mysterious, mystical, or sacred (at least *prima facie*), as those who aim to overcome the intellect through a leap suggest. The frontiers that bar the intellect's advance toward "reality," toward "God," are not archangels with flaming swords to be defeated in a fight, or infernal furies to be orphically enchanted. These frontiers are something much more prosaic: names. The last frontiers of the intellect, the point at which the intellect stops and no longer functions, are names of a certain type called proper names. The whole process called thought invests, in vain, from and against the proper names. The investigation of this type of word is therefore equivalent to the investigation of the limits of the intellect, and is equivalent to the investigation of the human condition, if we consider man as an intelligent being.

Traditional grammar, generally unconscious of its fundamental ontological function, classifies the words of a given language according to a supposed correspondence between words and "reality" (*adaequatio intellectus ad rem*). It distinguishes, for example, substantives, which correspond to "substances," adjectives, which correspond to "qualities," prepositions and conjunctions, which correspond to the "relations between substances," and verbs, which correspond to the "processes between substances." Traditional grammar is naive. It precedes the doubt of doubt and is illuminated by the grace of faith in the intellect and language. Its classification of words, the fruit of this naivety, needs to be abandoned. The best is to forget all of these devoted efforts as we come closer to the problem of the classification of words. However, it is evident that words need to be classified in some way. Words are the intellect's data. They are intellectual reality. The classification of words is the cosmic vision of reality. Classified words are a *Weltanschauung,* in the strict sense of the term.

If we look attentively at words, we may distinguish two types. The vast majority of words act as if they are implanted within the compost of language, organically thought and articulated within the mechanism of language. There are, however, words that seem unwilling to fit so organically; they demand an almost extra linguistic effort in order to be thought and articulated. When we think them, we feel a barrier, and when we articulate them, we are tempted to grunt, shout, or make a gesture. "This here," or "that there" are words of this type. Let us call this type "primary words," or "proper names." And let us call all the other words "secondary words." In order to distinguish the intellectual activity that involves thinking and articulating proper names from the activity that involves thinking and articulating secondary words, let us make a distinction between "to call" and "to converse." Proper names are "called" and secondary words are "conversed."

To call and to converse are, therefore, the two main intellectual activities. Proper names are called in order to be conversed, that is, to be transformed into secondary words. This transformation is gradual. As the proper names are conversed, they are transformed into secondary words that are always farther from their primary origin. The first stage of this transformation vaguely corresponds to the type of word that traditional grammar calls "substantive." These secondary words that are close to the proper names, and which serve as subjects and objects of phrases, are undergoing a transformation. It is worth observing this process a little closer.

Let us first consider the calling of a proper name. The field, which the intellect is, expands in the process in order to occupy a territory that was previously extra-intellectual. The result of this expansion is the emergence of a new word, which is the proper name that has been called. The process can be compared to the feeding process of amoebae. An amoeba emits a pseudopod toward something extra-amoebic and occupies it. Then, already within the amoebic reality, a vacuole is formed around this conquered something. This something is now part of the amoeba without having been incorporated into its metabolism. The vacuole closes and this something is gradually transformed into an amoeba, that is, into protoplasm, which is to say, it becomes amoebic reality. In this image, the emission of the pseudopod corresponds to the activity of calling, the vacuole corresponds to the proper name, the something inside the vacuole corresponds to the extra linguistic meaning of the proper name, and the digestion corresponds to the conversation. The amoeba as a whole corresponds to language as a whole. The amoeba's anatomy, which consists of vacuoles and protoplasm, corresponds to our classification of words into proper names and secondary words.

Insisting a little longer upon the image of the amoeba, we may say that the extra-amoebic territory, within which the amoeba emits its pseudopods, is the amoeba's becoming. The amoeba is the realization of this territory through protoplasmation. The amoeba expands into its potentialities, which are, from the amoeba's perspective, vacuoles in *statu nascendi*. However, a curious thing happens. Although the amoeba may occupy all possibilities with its pseudopods, and may form a vacuole around every occupied possibility, it cannot digest all of the possibilities. For example, a quartz crystal may be occupied and encapsulated within a vacuole, but it cannot be digested. All of the vacuole's contractions are in vain; the crystal shall always continue to be a foreign body within the amoeba's protoplasm. The best thing would be to expel it, unless the crystal may serve, precisely for being a foreign body, as a stimulant or catalyzer for the amoeba's metabolic processes.

Let us translate this image to the field of the intellect. Language may emit its callings into its becoming, which are the proper names in *statu nascendi,* in all possible directions. Everything that is possible may be called. These appeals shall always result in proper names. We may say that everything can be apprehended by the intellect. However, not everything may be transformed into secondary words. Not everything can be utilized as a subject or an object of a meaningful phrase. Not everything can be assimilated to the mechanism of language. Not everything can be comprehended. Inassimilable proper names shall always continue to be foreign bodies within the structure of language; they shall always continue to be bywords. A typical example of these bywords, these inassimilable proper names that are apprehended without ever being comprehended, is the word "God." Just as the chemical structure of the amoeba's protoplasm refuses to assimilate a quartz crystal, the structure of our languages refuses to assimilate the word "God." Nevertheless, precisely for being inassimilable, it may, perhaps, serve as a catalyzer for authentic linguistic processes. It may stimulate the conversation without ever being able to authentically participate in it.

Another emergent limitation of the intellect is that even though everything can be called a proper name, even though everything may be apprehended (at least in theory), not everything can be comprehended by the intellect; *not everything can be conversed.* We have arrived at this conclusion not because of some mystical speculation, but through an inter-intellectual observation of foreign bodies, which are proper names inapplicable to meaningful phrases. Being unable to serve as subjects or objects of meaningful phrases, these names do not transform into secondary words and remain bywords, that is, meaningless symbols, empty symbols. Nevertheless, they may still be, sometimes, of decisive importance for the intellectual process.

The act of calling is the intellect's only productive activity. Proper names are the products of this activity. The Scholastic quarrel between Nominalists and Realists, although extremely naive (since it is anterior to Cartesian doubt), proves that the distinctions between proper name and secondary word, and the productive power of the act of calling, have always been recognized by thinkers, even though confusedly, as being fundamental. Before proceeding with our investigation, let us clear our path from the detritus of this Scholastic quarrel. The Nominalists (the winners) affirm that proper names are "real," while secondary words are "aura." The Realists (the temporarily defeated) affirm that certain types of secondary words (the *universalia*) are equally "real." Let us disconsider the Platonic and Aristotelian background that hides behind these naive affirmatives, and let us consider only their formal aspect. Nominalists and their successors, the Empiricists, feel the experiential quality of the proper name, although they cannot grasp it intellectually, and feel the lack of this

54

quality in the case of secondary words. That is why they deny "reality" to secondary words. Nominalists and Empiricists are Existentialists in an embryonic stage. Realists feel that proper names are not ontologically different from the other words and cannot be rigorously differentiated from them since the intellectual process resides precisely in the transformation of proper names into secondary words. However, they do not resolve to concede the dignity of "reality" to all words, since they are committed, due to their naive faith, to an extra-linguistic reality. In a tacit agreement with traditional grammar, they consider words that this grammar calls "substantives" to be "real." Despite the naivety of the Scholastics, this excursion into the Middle Ages serves to illustrate the curious manner in which our thought, in its effort to overcome Descartes, returns to its pre-Cartesian origins.

The experiential quality that accompanies the productive activity of calling is known as "intuition." When the intellect calls something, it intuits this something. For the intellectual comprehension of intuition, it is necessary to liberate this concept from the extra-intellectual impurities that stick to it. Intuition is a synonym of the intellect's expansion into its potentialities. As I intuit something, I transform this something into a proper name, I realize this something within the intellect. However, since intuition is a borderline situation (*Grenzsituation*) for the intellect, the experience of the intellect's limits adheres to it: hence the origin of the extra-intellectual impurities that stick to it. In this sense we may say that the intellect expands intuitively. We may, however, define the intuition that results in the production of proper names better, since it is a productive intuition. We may call it "poetic intuition." The proper names are taken, through this intuitive activity, from the chaos of becoming in order to be put here (*hergestellt*), that is, in order to be brought into the intellect. To take in order to put is called, in Greek, *poiein*. Whoever takes in order to propose, therefore, whoever "produces," is the *poiétés*. The activity of calling, the activity that results in proper names is therefore the activity of poetic intuition. Poetry is the intellect's expansion. Poetry is a borderline situation of the intellect. Proper names are products of poetry. The almost extra-linguistic effort demanded by the effort to think and articulate proper names is the poetic effort. It is an effort because something is produced. It is poetic because new words are this something that is produced.

We may widen our concept of the intellect in the following manner: *it is the field in which two types of words occur: proper names and secondary words*. This field expands through poetic intuition, creating proper names to be converted into secondary words through conversation. We may distinguish two tendencies within the intellect's field, one centripetal and the other centrifugal. "Poetic intuition" is the centrifugal force, while "critical conversation" is the centripetal one. Proper names are the result of "poetic intuition," and the transformation of these names into secondary words, or their elimination from the intellect's field, is the result of "critical conversation." If the intellect is the field of doubt, we must say that doubt has two tendencies: the "intuitive," which expands the field of doubt, and the "critical," which consolidates it. Intuitive doubt creates the raw material for thought (proper names), and critical doubt converts this raw material into articulated organizations (meaningful phrases). Intuitive doubt is poetry and critical doubt is conversation. Poetry and conversation, two forms of doubt, are therefore, two forms of language. Two types of thoughts (linguistic organizations) occur within the intellect's field: poetic thoughts and conversational thoughts. Two types of thoughts occur within the intellect's field: "verses" and "converses."

Let us detain ourselves a little longer upon poetic thought, upon the type of thought that creates proper names, upon intuitive thought. Let us detain ourselves a little upon "verses." The "verse" is how the intellect precipitates itself upon the unarticulated chaos that circles it; it is the intellect's effort to break the fence of the chaos that limits the intellect. The "verse" is, therefore, language's borderline situation. Language attempts to overcome itself through the "verse." In the "verse," language attempts to articulate the inarticulable by turning the unthinkable thinkable, and by realizing nothingness. If this effort succeeds, the "verse" results in a proper name. The successful "verse" is the proclamation of a proper name. The "verse" wrenches a proper name from the chaos and verts[1] it toward the intellect. The "verse" is the act of verting a proper name. Therefore, it is not accurate to say that poetry represents an exclusively centrifugal force. The

---

1. In Portuguese, Flusser uses the verb *verter* from the Latin *vertere*, which means to turn or flip something. According to the OED, the verb "to vert" has the same meaning and etymology and is the root for invert, convert, pervert etc. Therefore, although it is no longer commonly used, I chose "to vert" in order to maintain Flusser's play on the words verse, version, conversion, inverted, and controverted, which all share this root. [TN]

57

"verse" calls a proper name, and in this particular phrase it is centrifugal. However, if the "verse" is successful, it proclaims the proper name and becomes centripetal in that particular phrase. The "verse" calls and proclaims; within it there is a conversion of 180 degrees. The poet, when he calls, has his back turned to the intellect, but as he proclaims, the poet turns toward the intellect. Poetic intuition, as it shocks against the inarticulable, wrenches the proper name from it and returns with this conquest to the field of articulation. This inverted and controverted situation of the "verse" forms a continuously recurring theme of humanity's myths. It is Moses that returns from Mount Sinai having wrenched the tablets from the unarticulated. It is Prometheus that returns from Mount Olympus to the valley of conversation, having wrenched fire from the unarticulated. It is the Rishis that return from on high, having wrenched the Veda from the unarticulated. These are three typical myths of the poetic activity. We can glimpse, in these myths, the experience of the "verse": it is a creative shock between the intellect and the unarticulated, a shock that is both an advance and a retrocession. The result of this shock is the enrichment of the intellect by a proper name. Language has gained, thanks to this shock, a new word.

The "verse" conserves, in its *Gestalt,* the stamp of this shock. The verb vibrates. The proper name scintillates, encrusted within the "verse" like a diamond in a mineral. Let us consider the "verse" with which Moses returned: "I am Yahweh, your God." There is an aura of vibration and light around the proper name "Yahweh." The proper name is "holy." Although the chosen example is an extreme one, since a large part of "Western civilization" spins around this "verse," we must say that every success-ful "verse" participates in this vibration and light. Every proper name is "holy." "Holiness" is the stamp of the shock that the intellect suffers when it faces the inarticulable, and every proper name conserves this stamp. "Holiness" is the experience of the limitation of the intellect and its absurd ability to overcome this limitation by calling and proclaiming proper names. Proper names are witnesses of the limitation and expandability of the intellect, and are, therefore, "holy."

The proper name, as the limitation and expansion of the intellect, is absurd. After all, what does "a successful verse" mean? It means the enrichment of language, but in no way does it mean the impoverishment of the inarticu-lable. Language expands but the chaos does not diminish. Poetry expands the territory of what is thinkable, but it does not diminish the territory of what is unthinkable. Poetry, being the borderline situation of language, bru-tally reveals the absurdity of the effort of thinking. The inarticulable, as it is penetrated by poetry, demonstrates what it is: inarticulable. The proper name reveals the insurmountable abyss that separates the intellect from the inarticulable precisely because it is a conquest of the intellect. Language grows, but the inarticulable remains untouched. The intellect is absurd. The proper name is palpable proof of the absurdity of the intellect. The proper name is palpable doubt. The proper name, being the *alpha* and the *omega* of the intellect, is the absurd cage within which we spin in small circles, like Rilke's panther. These small circles are the conversation. Let us consider the conversation.

Poetic intuition verts the "verse" toward language

so that it can be conversed. The centripetal process of conversation submits the "verse" to a critical analysis, it integrates the "verse" into the fabric of language through a critical explication, and thus it intellectualizes the "verse." It converts the "verse" into prose; it desecrates and profanes the "verse." Conversation is the process of critical explication, intellectualization, and profanation of the "verse." Conversation is the progressive realization of the project started by the "verse," toward language. The "verse" is the conversation's theme, its "topic." Conversation has the complete explication of the "verse" as an aim and progresses until it completely exhausts the "verse." Conversation progressively destroys the mystery of the "verse;" it destroys the stamp of the shock against the unarticulated. The "verse" is converted into prose through conversation. The prosaic manner of thought is the conversation's style. With the progress of conversation (if it is successful), the poetic mystery disappears and the prosaic climate prevails. Conversation, as the centripetal tendency of thought, is a distancing of thought from the inarticulable, and the concentration of thought upon itself. Conversation is the consolidation of thought. Thanks to conversation, thought becomes solid. As a critical analysis of the "verse," the conversation unfolds the "verse" into multiple layers of meaning, explicating the meaning that is hidden, contained, and implicit in the "verse." Conversation multiplies, ramifies, unfolds, and specializes thought. Thanks to conversation, thought becomes enriched. The intellectual possibilities hidden in the "verse" are revealed by conversation. Conversation realizes these possibilities. Conversation is the development of the possibilities involved in the "verse." Conversation is a historical process. *Sensu stricto,* conversation is identical to the concept "history," in its intellectually accessible meaning. The history of the world, the history of humanity, the history of a people, the history of an institution and an idea, the history of a person or of an event are, *sensu stricto,* histories of phrases of conversation, or the history of conversation as a whole. The "verse" happens *in illo tempore,* but as it is verted it originates an intellectually accessible time. Conversation is the intellectual aspect of time. The progress of conversation, "our" intellectual progress, is for us, identical to the progress of time. The past has been "conversed," the present "converses," and the future is "to be conversed." The meaning of progress is therefore the explication and the desecration, the intellectualization and the realization of the "verse." From this angle, "progress" and "decadence," "development" and "exhaustion" become synonyms.

From an intellectual point of view conversation is progress and development, and from poetry's borderline point of view, it is decadence and exhaustion. Formally speaking, conversation is a conversion of proper names into secondary words that are always farther from the proper name and always more abstract. Conversation is a process of abstraction. This abstraction is processed according to rules imposed by language, within which the conversation evolves. In the case of fusional languages, these rules may be identified, generally speaking, as "logic." In the conversation called "Western civilization," the rules of progress are logical (generally speaking). Logic, *sensu stricto,* applies to the last stage of conversation, to the last stage of abstraction, to the stage of mathematical language. The progress of the conversation called "Western Civilization" may be approached as the progress toward mathematics. It is the transformation of proper names into mathematical signs. Western conversation would exhaust itself if all the "verses" proposed to it were converted into mathematical equations. However, since poetic intuition never ceases to propose "verses" to the conversation, this exhaustion is unimaginable. Other types of languages obey other types of rules. Therefore, the history of these other conversations (for example the Chinese language, which is of the isolating type) has a different character than ours.

The transformation of proper names into more abstract words, which has, in our Western case, their transformation into mathematical signs as an aim, is a process that results in phrases of different levels of abstraction. The proper name proposed by the "verse" goes through these different levels of abstraction, through these different layers of language, in the course of their transformation. The conversation of the proper name is processed at different levels of abstraction, at different levels of intellectualization. The phrases formulated at these different levels are further "knowledge." Conversation produces knowledge. The sum of our knowledge is the sum of the phrases conversed at the different levels of abstraction. As they are transformed into secondary words, the proper names are progressively known. The progress of the conversation is the progress of knowledge. The transformation of a "verse" into a mathematical equation would be the perfect knowledge of this "verse."

The fragmentation of knowledge into different levels of abstraction represents an epistemological problem of the first order. The proper name is simultaneously being conversed at different levels of abstraction, therefore, at different levels of meaning. Each level of meaning corresponds to a mental (intellectual) discipline, with a slightly, or more than slightly, different methodology. In our Western case, each level of meaning corresponds to a different science, art, or ethics. The global vision of the different levels of meaning, which is the aim of epistemology, is opposed by the difficulties of translating from one level to another. The problem of knowledge is, essentially, a problem of translation. Specialized knowledge is the result of the translation of a proper name onto a given level of abstraction. Global knowledge would be the result of the translation of all levels of abstraction onto a neutral level, for example to the level of philosophical language. Formal Logic with its ad hoc invented language is the sign that epistemology is awakening to its function of translation in the current phase of Western conversation. This fact alone may be interpreted as an important symptom of the emptying of the meaning of "reality," of the intellectualization of the intellect, of the doubt of doubt, which characterizes the current stage of our conversation, and of which I spoke in the introduction to this book.

Poetic intuition never ceases to propose proper names to the conversation. The intuition of Western conversation shows no signs of weakening. From this angle there is no fear of an exhaustion of Western civilization. On the contrary, this intuition irrupts into the conversation at every level of meaning, which is intrinsically disquieting and difficult to evaluate. Poetic intuition exists within the layers of the different sciences, and even in the layer of mathematics. Proper names are proposed in these layers disguised as abstractions.

For example, in the layer of physics it is difficult to distinguish which are the secondary words as the result of conversation, and which are the proper names (such as, without a doubt, the word "field") as the result of poetic intuition. Western conversation shall not exhaust itself for the lack of intuition. The danger of stagnation comes from another direction. Our conversation has reached a stage where that which has been conversed is once again considered as that which is to be conversed. Conversation starts to double back on itself. Already articulated knowledge forms topics of conversation, and once again they become raw material to be known. Critical doubt turns against itself. This critique of critique (or "doubt of doubt," as I called it in the introduction), exemplified in this paragraph by symbolic logic, represents a vortex within Western conversation that threatens to submerge it into small talk. If this vortex, which is a self-intellectualization of the intellect, manages to attract all of the layers of meaning of our conversation to itself, as it has already done with a large part of the so-called "exact" sciences, our conversation shall spin on a fixed point. At such an advanced stage, poetic intuition shall serve for nothing, since the proper names shall no longer be converted into secondary words, and shall spin intact in a vicious circle. The doubt of doubt shall not allow for a naive doubt, a primary doubt, the doubt, therefore, which transforms proper names. The doubt of doubt, since it doubts doubt, is incapable of doubting the dubitable. Western conversation shall fall into a tedious repetition, into the Nietzschean "eternal return of the same." At this point the history of the West will have ended.

This doubling back of the conversation upon itself, which is a second-degree reflection, a secondary speculation, is essentially an abandonment of poetic intuition. Although it may result in an anti-intellectualism that is so characteristic of several current tendencies, this is not an anti-intellectualism that searches for the origins (poetic intuition) of the intellect, but which seeks to leap out of the vicious circle, which for these thinkers is the intellect. It is within this abandonment of poetic intuition that the fundamental danger of the doubt of doubt resides. It rejects the intellect *in toto*, including the centrifugal phase, the poetic phase of the intellect, in order to suicidally dive into "experience," into the unarticulated. The doubt of doubt is anti-poetry. It does not precipitate itself *over* but *into* the unarticulated. It becomes mute. This mutism is the abyss that has opened up before us.

The proper name, this mysterious source of language, this memento of the limitation of the intellect, is at the same time a memento of the function of the intellect. The doubt of doubt, bedazzled by the limitation of the intellect, which is the proper name, forgets the function of the intellect, which is the same as that of the proper name. The doubt of doubt is the result of the loss of faith in doubt, of the loss of faith in the possibility to critique the proper name: not believing in the possibility to critique the proper name, it paradoxically abandons the proper name. The way out of this situation, in my view, is not to regain faith in doubt, but the transformation of the doubt of doubt into faith in the proper name as the source of doubt. In other words: it is to accept the limitations of the intellect, simultaneously accepting the intellect as the method, *par excéllence,* through which we shock against the inarticulable. This acceptance would not only be the overcoming of intellectualism, but also of anti-intellectualism, which would allow the continuation of Western conversation, although in a more humble climate. It would allow us to continue weaving the wonderful web that is Western conversation, although without the hope of capturing the rock of the inarticulable in this web. It would be the recognition of this web's function: not to capture the rock, but to envelop it. It would be the recognition that the intellect is not an instrument for the domination of chaos, but an ode in praise of the indomitable. The proper name is not the result of an intellectual effort, but of a shock between the intellect and the indomitable. The proper name is the synthesis of the intellect and the all-different. The proper name, and by "power of attorney" every word, is the holy Name. The recognition of this mysterious source of every word may be the beginning of a new sense of "reality;" a rebirth of a sense of proximity to the all-different within the intellect; a rebirth of a sense of the intellect's function, and in this sense, of the function of our existence.

IV. On Proximity

Bedazzled before the all-different, oppressed and crushed by it, but also propelled toward it by love and the desire for union, the nascent intellect prostrates itself. More precisely, the prostration before the all-different is the birth of the intellect. It is difficult to grasp the tremendous mystery that is the birth of the intellect. As we attempt to do it, we tremble, because it is the attempt to climb down to our roots. In *Faust*, it is what Goethe calls "the climb down to the mothers." Despite our trembling (which is fear and euphoria), this climb down is necessary for whoever, like us in this undertaking, desires to conquer a new sense of the function of the intellect.

It happened *in illo tempore*, and it is always happening: that which is all-different from us, as thinking beings, turns against itself in order to face itself. We have very intimate knowledge of such fundamental happening because we, as thinking beings, are precisely this turning action of the all-different against itself. The all-different is all-different from us due to this turning action. We are the alienation of the all-different from itself. We, as thinking beings, are the doubt that the all-different conjures up by turning against itself. Since we are the doubt, we lean toward the question: Why did this turning happen? Why does it continue to happen? This is the original question; it demands to know the origin of things as well as our origin. However, as we are alienated from the all-different, we are incapable not only of answering it, but also of formulating the question properly. The word "why" is typical of the doubt that we are. Causality is a category of "pure reason." It cannot project itself out of the field of doubt. It cannot project itself out of the intellect that we are as thinking beings. The all-different, for not being subjected to intellectual categories, cannot be studied through them. The intellect is not an instrument for the study of the all-different. Our question is not legitimate. Therefore, it cannot be formulated. The origin of things, and our origin as thinking beings in opposition to things, is unarguable, it cannot be discussed. The origin of language (which is the origin of things and the origin of our opposition to them) cannot be discussed. By leaning toward this question, the intellect leans toward the absurd.

Therefore, although we cannot ask "why" we are alienated from the all-different, we may attempt to ask "how." We may formulate this question because we have a method to answer it at our disposal. How did this alienation from the all-different happen *in illo tempore,* and how is it happening today? We should be able to answer this question, because this alienation is happening due to our existence as thinking beings, it is happening because of us, through us, and thanks to us. To say that we are as we are is to say that this alienation is happening. There are several ways to formulate and answer this question, and some of them are consecrated by Western conversation. "*Cogito ergo sum*" is the Cartesian formulation. "*Propter admirationen enim et nunc et primo homines principiabant philosophari,*" is the Aristotelian formulation. Both the Cartesian and the Aristotelian "verses" are articulations of the alienation of the all-different from itself. The investigation that preceded this chapter opens the possibility of a slightly different articulation of both "verses" mentioned. Our articulation shall certainly be more modest, but it shall have the advantage of not having been "conversed" by Western conversation. It shall therefore conserve the stamp of the all-different, the stamp which Western conversation has, in large part, erased from the face of the two majestic "verses," which have already been mentioned, and which have already been transformed into prose.

When the all-different faces itself (in other words, when we stand before the all-different), it is in a situation of self-expulsion. The awareness of this expulsion is at the root of our awareness of ourselves. We are, as thinking beings, fundamentally expelled beings. We are groundless. Our oldest myths mirror the pre-intellectual "knowledge" of this groundlessness. (The expulsion from paradise.) The mystics, in trying to articulate this awareness, speak of "spiritual exile" and Jewish mysticism even knows the expression "*galuth shel ha shekinah*" (the exile of the Holy Spirit). Existential thought gives expression to this awareness in saying that "we are thrown" (*geworfen*). Our question may be formulated, therefore, in the following manner: How was the all-different expelled by itself, and how is that happening today? Our answer shall be: This expulsion is the formulation of the proper name. The proper name is the frightened shout, the exclamation of admiration, the adoration and the longing by the all-different for itself. The proper name is the expulsion (expression) of the all-different out of itself. The proper name is

69

the doubt that the all-different nurtures for itself, and it is the attempt to overcome this doubt, the attempt to return to itself. The proper name is an "*Abkehr*," "*Einkehr*," and the attempt at "*Heimkehr*" (an estrangement, a pause, and an attempt at a homecoming).

Therefore, that which is all-different from us confronts itself through the proper name. The place where this happens, the place where proper names emerge, the place where the all-different faces itself, is within us, it is our intellect. Our intellect is where the estrangement, the pause, and the attempt at a homecoming of the all-different happens. Therefore, the intellect is not a mirror of the all-different, like those who establish an adequation between intellect and "thing" imagine. If we wish to keep the image of the mirror, we have to say that the intellect is a blind mirror, although it wants to be a mirror. In its prostration, in its admiration, and in its fear before the all-different, the intellect is a frustrated attempt at being a mirror. The intellect faces the all-different through the proper name, however, without being able to see the all-different. The intellect is a frustrated and desperate attempt to see. Paradoxically: if the intellect were successful in its attempt, if it managed to see "the thing," this would also be the end of the intellect. The vision of the "thing" is a fusion between intellect and "thing," and the disappearance of the intellect. The vision of the "thing," consciously aimed at by the mystics, and unconsciously by the epistemologists, is our end as thinking beings. If we ever manage to see the "thing," we will cease to be ourselves.

We may, therefore, translate the two classic "verses" mentioned above in the following manner: "*Cogito ergo sum.*" = "I do not see 'the thing,' therefore I am." ("To think" = "To be exiled from the 'thing'; to be blind in face of the 'thing.'") "*Propter admirationen enim et nunc et primo homines principiabant philosophari.*" = "Through the admiration of the 'thing' man started to philosophize (that is, to become a thinking being) both in our time and *in illo tempore.*" ("Admiration" = "the attempt to see" and "to philosophize" = "to not be able to see; to be exiled from the 'thing.'") To reformulate Descartes: "I have proper names, therefore I am." To reformulate Aristotle: "Through proper names, man started to become what he is not, both in our time and *in illo tempore.*"

It is necessary to grasp this action of thinking and admiration that is the proper name to the utmost (this blindness and attempt to see, which the proper name is) if we wish to grasp, although nebulously, the emergence of the intellect, or "how" language irrupted. In the previous chapter there was an attempt to appreciate the proper name as the limitation of the intellect, as the frontier of language. The proper name has been described as the barrier against which the intellect shocks in its attempt to precipitate itself upon the all-different, upon the inarticulable. In other words: the proper name has been appreciated from within the intellect, from secondary words; it has been appreciated as the treetop of the tree of our intellect. Now we need a mental reversal, an effort to appreciate the proper name as the root of this tree, as the source from which the intellect springs. We need to mentally cancel secondary words, to cancel "putting into brackets" every conversation that emerges from proper names; we need to put ourselves inside the proper name just as we are, without any posterior comments about the intellect. We need to make an introspective effort. Since, in this effort, we must dispense with every "prosaic" conversation, we are forced to appeal to allegories in order to describe the proper name as it presents itself when seen from within.

Introspection reveals the proper name as a lightning bolt that tears the extra-intellectual, extra-linguistic darkness that we face and to which we are opposed. The bolt is of such luminosity that it makes nothing of the "thing" visible, which we experientially feel is hidden in the darkness. The light from the bolt that is the proper name, obfuscates the "things," it does not shed light upon them. Although the proper name wishes to illuminate the darkness from which it emerged, it illuminates nothing except itself. Although the proper name wishes to "signify" the "thing," it signifies nothing but itself. Before the lightening bolt everything was darkness. Intellectually speaking, everything was nothing. After the bolt struck the darkness disappeared within the luminosity, the luminosity annihilated nothingness. It also annihilated the "thing" that it wanted to illuminate. This luminosity (*Lichtung*) that is the loss of the "thing," is our nascent intellect; it is what we are. Our exile from the "thing" and our longing for the "thing" is precisely the bedazzlement by the light that we are; this impenetrable light blinds us. The intellect is self-destructive. The intellect is absurd.

The proper name – this lightening bolt that tears the darkness, and the intellect, this luminous wall woven out of lightening bolts that covers (*vorstellt*) the darkness – leans toward the darkness. The proper name oversees the darkness. The proper name wants to dissolve itself in the darkness by illuminating it. The proper name wants to "signify" the thing, and the intellect "adores" the all-different. The proper name "adores" the thing, and the intellect "adores" the all-different. (To adore = to speak toward.) In this sense the proper name is adoration. Effectively, it is the essence of adoration; it is adoration itself. *The intellect, or language, inclined as it is toward the all-different, is essentially an adoration of the all-different.* The intellect is a prayer. However, although the proper name leans toward the darkness, although it wants to "signify" the darkness, and although it adores the darkness, the proper name is opposed to the darkness. The proper name is essentially the opposition to the darkness. It is the all-different of the darkness. The proper name is charged with an energy that will give origin to the intellect, that is, to language, with its ordered and organized structure. The proper name is the seed of order. The darkness is a stranger to order, it is completely different from order. From the intellectual perspective the darkness is the chaos. The proper name is frightened of the chaos. The proper name is frightened of the all-different. Even though the proper name wants to fuse with the chaos in order to illuminate it, the proper name is frightened of being swallowed up by the chaos, and of falling back into the chaotic mumbling of the unarticulated. The all-different, which the proper name adores, is frightening.

Thus, adoration and fear are the climate (*Stimmung*) of the proper name, the climate of the emergence of the intellect. Adoration and fear, prostration and primordial tremor (*Urschauder*), are the "*Stimmung*" that gives origin to language. Language is the progressive articulation (always renewed by the emergence of proper names) of the primordial tremor, of that primordial tremor through which the all-different alienates itself from itself. The primordial tremor ("*myterium tremendum*") is the "*Stimmung*" that makes language tremble and what originates its structure. Vibrating and trembling before the all-different, language orders itself. It is in this mysterious sense that language *concords* with the all-different. Language vibrates when faced with the all-different; language is its string. Language forms a trembling accord with the all-different. Although there is no accordance between language and the all-different, there is this mysterious accord, which is the ordered vibration of language. Pythagoras and the Mystagogues searched for this accord in geometry, Orpheus played it on the lyre, and Pan on the flute. In this sense, language is the voice of the all-different. Although it does not "describe" or explain the all-different, language articulates it. Language is the cry and appeal of the all-different against itself. In this sense language corresponds to the all-different. This is the climate of language. In German, this mysterious character of language becomes clearer: "climate" = "*Stimmung*," "accordance" = "*stimmen*," "to tune a string" = "*stimmen*," and "voice" = "*Stimme*." However, in Portuguese, what is unthinkable in German, becomes thinkable: Language is in accord [*acorde*], but not in accordance [*acôrdo*] with the all-different. There is an abyss between language and the unarticulated, which no accordance can bridge.

The accord that accompanies the alienation that gives origin to language happened *in illo tempore* and is still happening every time a new proper name appears. Language emerged *in illo tempore* and is continuously emerging. Language is the eternal repetition of its origin, the eternal re-enactment of the primordial accord that accompanies alienation. In language the primordial accord always sounds current; it is always present. *Language is essentially festive. Effectively, language is the essence of the feast.* To say that we are thinking beings is to say that we participate in a feast. Thought is the eternal feast of the alienation of the all-different from itself. Every human myth and ritual is, essentially, an individual phase, an inferior and partial feast, of this single, enormous feast of alienation that thought is. These inferior and partial feasts sometimes emphasize the phase of estrangement, sometimes the phase of pause, and sometimes the phase of attempting a homecoming. They sometimes emphasize one or another facet of the proper name. Language, or thought, is the collection of all feasts, that is, of all myths and rituals. More precisely: language is the source from which every myth and ritual springs. Language is the master-feast.

Every proper name is a myth. Every proper name carries the primordial shock of the alienation of the all-different from itself. Every proper name vibrates (is in accord) with the all-different. This vibration, this accord, is the ritual through which the proper name will be transformed into a secondary word. The vibration of the proper name is the ritual through which conversation transforms the verse into prose. Language is a feast whose myths are the proper names, and whose ritual is the conversation. Conversation is the ritualization and demythologization of proper names. *The intellect may be defined as the field in which myths happen (proper names), and as the field in which these myths are demythologized by the ritual of conversation, that is, by grammatical rules.* The intellect may be defined as the field of the feast. Language is the feast of the ritual demythologization of proper names. The intellect is the field of doubt because it is the field of the demythologization of myths. To think is to doubt, because to think is the ritual of demythologization. That which was called the centripetal tendency of language in the preceding chapter, may now be redefined as the ritualistic tendency of the feast that is language. That which was called the centrifugal tendency of language may be redefined as a tendency toward the myth of the feast that is language. Poetic intuition produces myths (proper names) and conversation demythologizes them through the ritual of grammar. Poets are mythologists (the raconteurs of myths); critics ritualize myths. Poets are prophets, and critics are the priests of the feast that is language.

The proper name, the myth of the feast of thought, is the point in which the intellect comes close to the inarticulable. The proper name is a myth because it seeks to articulate the inarticulable. The proper name is the proximity to the inarticulable. In the proper name we are close to the inarticulable and the inarticulable is close to us. In thought we fete this proximity. Thought is an exuberant, euphoric, terrifying and frightening experience because it fetes the proximity to the inarticulable. The ritual of thought (grammar) orders, organizes, and makes bearable, the exuberance and terror of thought. To be bearable, the world of the intellect is an organized cosmos, a well-ordered feast. The disorganization of thought, the deritualization of the feast of proximity, is madness. In madness the feast of proximity becomes an orgy. In madness the ordered vibration of the proper name becomes orgiastic convulsion. In madness, thought is no longer in accord, but in discord with the all-different. In madness, "*stimmt etwas nicht*" (something is not in accordance). Madness is an orgy; it is the disintegration of the intellect. Madness, for being orgiastic is not properly festive. Madness is an inauthentic feast. Madness is not in proximity of the inarticulable, but on the way toward diving into it. Madness is the inauthentic poetic intuition.

Conversation is the ritual critique of the proper name; it is the ritual explication of the proper name. Conversation is in proximity to the inarticulable because it spins around the proper name. Conversation is a ritual dance around the inarticulable. The inarticulable that vibrates in the proper name is the center, the "meaning" of the conversation's dance. Conversation is the unfolding of this vibration. Authentic conversation is an ode in praise of the inarticulable that vibrates in the proper name. Authentic conversation is the ritual prayer that explains the adoration that is the proper name. The proper name is the adoration of the inarticulable, and authentic conversation is the prayer around this adoration. The intellect adores (intuitive phase) and prays (critical phase). Language is ritual adoration and prayer. By adoring the inarticulable, and praying about it, the intellect is in proximity to the inarticulable.

Western conversation reached a stage of ritualization in which prayer no longer prays about the inarticulable, but about itself. At the current stage of Western conversation, the ritual of the feast of thought has become its myth. Prayer adores itself and prays about itself. As proper names appear, they are no longer accepted as myths to be ritualized, but as rituals to be included in an ever-growing ritual. The ritual is the aim of the inauthentic feast that is today's Western conversation. Conversation has become inauthentic, it has become small talk. The exuberant and terrifying experience has evaporated. Conversation has become tedious and nauseating; it spins in circles without a center; it has no "meaning"; it does not pray about the inarticulable, but about itself; it is self-mythologizing; it is a topsy-turvy madness; it is what I called the "doubt of doubt" in the introduction. At this stage of small talk, the intellect becomes self-sufficient because it has lost its center, that is, the inarticulable. It is distant from proximity. Small talk is the profanation of the feast of thought. In small talk everything is profane, therefore nauseating. The world of small talk is a completely ritualized and de-mythologized cosmos, which absurdly has ritual as myth; it is total intellectualization, which has as a consequence, the abandonment of the intellect, emptied of its festive content and turned nauseating.

Current scientific conversation is a beautiful example of this small talk. Science no longer prays about "reality," about the inarticulable, but about itself. The proper names that poetic intuition verts upon the scientific conversation (for example, "meson" or "antiproton") no longer adore the inarticulable, but the ritual of scientific conversation. Science tends to be self-sufficient; it tends to be nauseating. The festive experience tends to evaporate from scientific conversation, which tends to dive into the topsy-turvy madness, into the madness of small talk.

78

Science no longer doubts "reality," but itself. The ritual of science is its myth. Science is distancing itself from the proximity to the inarticulable, to the all-different. Science is profaning itself. Science is becoming a dance without a center. Science is distancing itself from "meaning." At this level, Western conversation is threatened with stagnation and a Wittgensteinian mutism. What has been said in relation to science may be said, with equal pertinence, in relation to art, especially in relation to so-called abstract art. Ritual becomes myth; art profanes itself and becomes nauseating. The same may be said in relation to the other levels of today's Western conversation, perhaps with less pertinence, but with an equally frightening validity. We are watching an emptying out of the festive character of Western thought; a profanation of this thought; a distancing from "meaning." Western thought is becoming distant from the inarticulable. Western thought is becoming distant from the proximity to the all-different, in order to turn against itself. The primordial fear, the prostration before the all-different, and the alienation of the all-different from itself that gave origin to the intellect, are *toto coelo distantes* from Western thought. Western thought is submerged in small talk.

Today's super-intellectualism and anti-intellectualism are the consequences of this submersion. However, they are not the only alternatives in light of the present state of things. A reevaluation of the intellect as the field of the feast opens a third alternative. The festive character of thought is veiled within a primitive stage of Western conversation. The participants of the feast of thought are not aware, at this stage, that they are taking part in a feast. The Australian dancer is not aware that he is taking part in a ritual through which the myth of the kangaroo is being ritualized. He cannot distinguish "feast" from the all-different. As he dances he *is* the kangaroo, he does not *signify* the kangaroo. At a more advanced stage of the conversation the festive character of thought is revealed. Epistemological problems of language progressively emerge. The abyss that separates thought from the inarticulable becomes visible. And this progressive revealing of the festive character of thought results in the total alienation of thought that characterizes the current stage of Western conversation. The revealing of the festive character of thought destroys the very character it reveals. But it is possible to consciously participate in a feast. It is possible to participate in a feast while knowing that it is a feast. It is possible to know of the abyss that separates the feast from the all-different, and to know, at the same time, of the proximity reached in the feast. It is possible to adore the all-different and pray about the all-different, knowing of the abyss that separates us from the all-different. This humility, this knowledge of our own limitations is possible. Through the progress of conversation we irrevocably know that we cannot subjugate the all-different through our intellect (something that the Australian dancer does not know). But we also know that the intellect is our way, as thinking beings, to adore and pray over the all-different (something that the Australian dancer also does not know). From instrument of power, the intellect transforms itself into an instrument of adoration. This seems to me to be the true overcoming of magic. This seems to me to be true intellectualism.

Our civilization, a fruit of Western conversation, would suffer a deep alteration of content, although not in an immediate way, as a result of this overcoming of magic, of this true intellectualism. But our instruments and institutions would not be immediately abandoned because of that. However, instead of being considered as magical instruments and institutions, that is, destined to conquer the all-different, they would be considered as ritual instruments and institutions, that is, dedicated to the adoration of the all-different. The machine would no longer be an instrument of conquest, but a ritually explicated example of the vibration that the proper name (which originated it) suffered in the shock of alienation from the all-different. The State would no longer be an institution of conquest, but an example of the mysterious way in which the primordial vibration is ritually explicated in the course of the conversation. In this way, the mythologization of the machine and the State would be overcome (which is, essentially, the mythologization of a ritual). The pragmatization of the instrument and the institution would also be overcome; this pragmatization, which makes civilization so anti-festive, so nauseating. Once the ritual of our civilization is demythologized, and once its praxis is depragmatized, our civilization shall once again be an authentic feast, and to take part in it shall be a festive activity.

The scientific activity that is so characteristic of our civilization would become a conscious prayer, a religious activity. It would no longer endeavor to explicate and foresee "reality," as it attempted in the past. Nor would it be a self-sufficient discipline in search of a perfect internal consistency, as it tends to be today. It would become a fundamentally aesthetic intellectual effort, an attempt to compose a perfect prayer, a prayer in praise of the unarticulated. Knowing itself to be in accord with the all-different through the shock of the primordial fear, this activity would no longer be "true," but in accordance (*stimmen*). In the course of the conversation, the classificatory and specializing division of Western thought (so characteristic and so nefarious) would tend toward being overcome. Science would tend toward being comprehended as a typical form of art, of applied art, of "engaged" art, for being committed to the all-different.

In the course of the conversation, our civilization would not only change its content, but also its form. The center of interest would shift from science without abandoning it, and new, for now unimaginable, centers of interest would open up. The technological phase of our society would be overcome. As totally unpredictable, the intellectual activity would once again become an adventure. The feast that is thought would once again become dramatic in the Greek sense of the word. The current phase of our conversation would appear, then, as a transition phase of the uninterrupted and always renewed feast of Western thought. In other words: the religious foundation, upon which Western thought and every other thought, is based, and which recently crumbled, would be rediscovered and reformulated. Westerners would continue to adore and pray about the all-different in their typical manner, which had already produced such beautiful and majestic results in the past. Western thought would return to the proximity of the all-different.

V. ON SACRIFICE

Western conversation could develop in the manner sketched out in the previous chapter if our attitude in relation to the intellect were modified. This modification is, however, highly problematic. Effectively, as optimistic as we may be, we will have great difficulty in discovering symptoms for an eventual realization of this modification. On the contrary, symptoms that denote an intensification of the plunge into small talk abound. The mythologization of the ritual of conversation advances in all levels of language, and is paradoxically accompanied by a cynical pragmatism. We are, in other words, watching the development of an opportunistic dogmatism. The mythologization of ritual means the dogmatization of thought. Pragmatism in the face of the products of thought means opportunism. Both are symptoms of a stagnation of the thinking process. Thought loses the elasticity that characterizes it in its stage of authentic conversation, the elasticity that allows for a game, free of commentaries about the verse proposed by poetic intuition, within the rules of the ritual of grammar. On the other hand, thought progressively becomes more rigorous, it acquires precision and specialization in an ever more restrictive sense: *rigor mortis*. This is the dogmatic side of small talk.

Simultaneously, thought loses the enthusiasm and aggressiveness that characterize it in its stage of authentic conversation, the enthusiasm which allows for a disinterested critical activity. On the other hand, it acquires an apologetic flavor, and exegesis is gradually substituting critique. It becomes not so much a question of explicating the verse proposed by intuition, but of applying it. This is the pragmatic and opportunistic side of small talk. This nefarious combination between dogmatism and pragmatism accelerates the decadence of Western conversation, because it is both soporific and narcotic. The dance of Western conversation around lost meaning realizes itself, thanks to these combinations, in increasingly smaller and ever more rigorously delineated circles. We are always conversing more rigorously about less. And we are conversing not in order to converse, but to polemicize. We are not critics but propagandists. Effectively, Western conversation is not developing, but propagating. It is propagating toward mutism.

The alternative delineated in the previous chapter seems non-existent. The conscious return to the proximity of the all-different does not seem to come into the game of currently operative tendencies. This apparent blindness before the function of the intellect is easy to explain. The recognition of the intellect as an instrument of adoration and prayer implies an enormous sacrifice. In order for us to evaluate the enormity of this sacrifice, it is necessary to go back to the Middle Ages, when it seemed that the intellect had been thus recognized. After all, is it not true that in those times philosophy was considered as a servant of theology, therefore, the intellect as the servant of faith?

Let us consider the position of the intellect in this medieval conception a little closer. From this position, the scene was dominated by faith, which was a kind of immediate and extra-intellectual vision that God concedes to us by the power of His grace. The intellect was considered as a kind of lantern that God gave us in order to illuminate the "truths" revealed by the solar rays of faith with a little more detail. Certainly a very good lantern, since it was a Divine gift, but incomparably less intense than the rays of faith, and incomparably less meaningful. The Middle Ages verified, with a certain level of surprise and dislike, that the intellect did not always agree with faith, and therein was a problem. The orthodox answer to this problem was to sacrifice the intellect in favor of faith in instances of disagreement. It was a considerable sacrifice, since the intellect was of Divine origin, but it was a reasonable sacrifice, since it conserved the most valuable part. The heterodox answer to this problem was the sacrifice of faith in favor of the intellect. This was an enormous and absurd sacrifice. It substituted faith with doubt which is the intellect, and in this way, threw man, as a thinking being, into the sea of uncertainties that is the Modern Age. However, as this book attempts to suggest, this sacrifice was not as great as it may have seemed at first glance. In this sacrifice, faith took refuge within the intellect in order to be conserved intestinally. Cartesian doubt is this conservation of faith within the intellect.

Faith in the medieval sense of the word no longer exists in the present stage of Western conversation. It no longer exists in its manifested medieval form, or in its hidden form within the intellect. From our perspective, this faith is nothing more than the unawareness of the festive character of language, of the festive and abysmally distant character of thought before the all-different. This faith is definitely lost. Lack of knowledge is something that cannot be regained. Even though it has been "corrected" (*gestimmt*), this faith is not for us. The longing for this faith at the current stage of Western conversation is one more symptom of our dogmatic and opportunistic anti-intellectualism.

The history of Western conversation proves that the absurd sacrifice of faith in favor of the intellect was productive, while the reasonable sacrifice of the intellect in favor of faith was sterile. This was because it is within the character of a sacrifice to be absurd. The sacrifice, of recognizing the intellect as an instrument of adoration and prayer, which imposes itself upon us is, however, a more absurd and greater sacrifice. We cannot sacrifice the intellect to any faith, since we do not have faith. And we cannot surreptitiously conserve something of the intellect in the sacrifice, as the Middle Ages conserved something of faith. To rephrase, the new attitude proposed in these considerations imposes the sacrifice of the intellect in exchange for nothing. Therefore, it is not surprising that this attitude is not easily observable in the game of current tendencies. Attitudes of sacrifice of the intellect in exchange for experience, or for the Will to Power, or for instinct, abound. Yes, these may be easily observed. But the attitude of sacrifice of the intellect in exchange for a ridiculously diminished intellect, the attitude of humiliation of the intellect without compensation, is an attitude that cannot, understandably, attract a multitude of adepts.

However, this absurd attitude imposes itself, if the analysis of the intellect carried out in this book has any validity.

The sacrifice is an integral part of the feast. In a way the sacrifice is the culminating point of the feast. In the sacrifice, the absurdity that thought is, in its most evident expression, is reached. The sacrifice is the reduction of the absurdity of thought to the absurd. The sacrifice of the intellect in favor of the intellect would be the essence of absurdity, therefore, the essence of the sacrifice. The absurd sacrifice of the absurd in favor of the absurd would be, by the principle of double negation, the annulment (*Aufhebung*) of the absurd. The sacrifice of the intellect in favor of the intellect seems to me, therefore, to be the highest intellectual honesty. It seems to me, in other words, the highest sanity. It is the overcoming of the doubt of doubt through the acceptance of a horizon of doubt. Beyond this horizon, which is the horizon of the intellect, everything is indubitable, in the sense of not even being able to be doubted, and not even the doubt about it can be doubted. This is the horizon of the thinkable. Beyond this horizon the doubt of doubt dissolves, because the doubt of doubt is, in the last analysis, the non-acceptance of the horizon. The acceptance of the proper name as horizon dissolves the doubt of doubt on both sides of the horizon, and substitutes it for the sacrifice of the intellect in favor of the intellect; for the sacrifice of the doubt of doubt in favor of doubt; for the sacrifice of thinking about thought in favor of thinking about the all-different.

What are we sacrificing in this festive sacrifice? In the last analysis, we are sacrificing the aim to which Western conversation committed itself, and which it consciously and subconsciously pursued for at least three thousand years. This aim may be described, within the context of this book, in the following manner: Western conversation is, as in every conversation, the result of an alienation from the inarticulable. Its aim is the overcoming of this alienation through the articulation of the inarticulable. Western thought has as an aim to make the unthinkable thinkable and thus to eliminate it. The Western intellect has total intellectualization as an aim. It is in this sense that we must say that the West is idealist in all of its manifestations, including the so-called "materialistic" ones. This idealistic, totalitarian aim distinguishes Western conversation from all others, although it is highly difficult for us Westerners to grasp the aim of the conversations that are strange to us. Every conversation springs from a distinct proximity and vibrates differently. Every conversation is a distinct feast. As Westerners, we cannot authentically participate in another feast whose myths and whose rituals are strange to us. However, we may translate. Translation is an ambiguous concept. It means a ritual of the Western feast, when it refers to the passage from one language to another, or from one layer of meaning to another within the same language. It means a myth (a proper name) when it refers to the passage from one conversation to another. For us, Westerners, strange conversations like those of the Chinese or the Eskimo for example, are myths. As such, they are incorporated into our conversation and subjected to our ritual. What we think about them is thought through the Western ritual. They do not contain extra-conversational value, just as they do not contain anything of what we think. With this salvo we may reaffirm that the aim of Western conversation is different from the aims of all other conversations in the sense that it is idealistic and totalitarian. The "homecoming" that Western conversation aims at is not the return of the prodigal son, but the return of the exiled rebel turned conqueror. Western conversation has a heroic aim. Western conversation is proud. The sacrifice, which imposes itself, is the sacrifice of pride.

At least two fundamental myths of Western conversation prefigure this sacrifice; they are its project. They are the myth of Prometheus and the myth of the Tower of Babel. It seems as if Western conversation has reached the phase of the realization of this project, initiated by these two myths. The time has come for the sacrifice foreseen in the project of the feast's ritual. The time has come for the great sacrifice, compared to which, all other sacrifices have been nothing more than preparatory rites. The time has come for the Caucasus, and the confusion of languages. Nietzsche describes the approaching of the hour of the sacrifice by saying that "every day it is getting colder." This is the apocalyptic cold, and the festive and ritual silence that precedes the sacrifice. The feast seems to come to a standstill. The participants, overwhelmed by fear, ritually turn their backs to the sacrificial altar, to the "meaning" of the feast, and, burying their faces in their hands, they continue, as if automatically, to carry out the steps of the dance in increasingly more restricted circles. The sacrifice to be carried out is exceedingly horrible, and is relegated to oblivion by the participants of the feast. This seems to me to be one way of interpreting the prevailing symptoms today.

The pride to be sacrificed has reached gigantic proportions in the course of the feast. It became gigantic in every layer of meaning. The ritual of the feast converted the Promethean fire and the Babylonian tower into exact science, technology, depth psychology, planned economy, and abstract art. It is in this enlarged and ritualized form that the pride, into which the Western intellect has been converted, must be sacrificed. The sacrifice that imposes itself is a holocaust. However, it was already foreseen in the feast's project. It had already been consummated *in illo tempore* when the proper names "Prometheus" and "Babel" emerged. Prometheus has already been sacrificed, and the tower has already been destroyed. The hour of the sacrifice has come, as it always does at this point in the feast. The terror spreads among the participants, as it always does at this point in the feast. The feast seems to come to an end, as it always does at this point. The feast is in danger of rupturing, as it always is at this point. The danger is real, as it always is at this point. But the sacrifice, as it prefigures in the feast's project, is possible, as it always is at this point.

The feast's ritual is not rigid. It obeys its own *momentum* as it unfolds. The grammar of Western conversation is always in flux. The unfolding of our feast is unpredictable. To wish to predict the unfolding of the feast is to want to completely explicate the proper names that were proposed as a theme. It is to want to completely predicate the subjects and objects into which the proper names were converted in the course of the feast. The unfolding of the feast is identical to an explication of proper names. To wish to predict this unfolding is to want to overcome it metaphysically. The feast, being the explication of proper names, is its own explication as it unfolds. To wish to predict the unfolding of the feast is to want the absurd. To think about the unfolding of the feast is to participate in it. To think about the "future" unfolding of the feast is absurd. In thinking about the "future" unfolding of the feast we are realizing such a future, we are transforming the future into the present. The "future" of the feast is the not yet explicated, the yet to be conversed, and by definition, the as yet inconversible.

We cannot, therefore, say if the sacrifice shall be carried out. We may, however, affirm that as we think about the sacrifice, we are contributing toward its realization. Western conversation is a feast of many participants, although not as many as it may seem at first sight. The majority of intellects apparently engaged in this conversation do not effectively participate in the feast. This majority is made up of inauthentic intellects that have fallen into small talk. These intellects are not authentic fields of doubt, but fields through which mere detritus of doubt, or "cliches," pass like meteors. These inauthentic intellects are nothing more than depositories for the refuse of Western conversation. They are, in the best of cases, cutout figures or marionettes of the feast. Even so, several intellects participate in the feast; they think, critique, and convert verses into prose. The unfolding of the feast depends on all of them. All of them contribute toward the enlargement, the gradual widening, of the fabric of the conversation, and toward the constant modification of its structure. This book also contributes toward it. In its modest and very limited scope, this book contributes toward the realization of the sacrifice. In this sense, it is framed in the feast's ritual. It is filled with the same fear that dominates the current phase of the feast, and trembles from the same cold. This book is among the ones that are conscious of the primordial origin of this fear and trembling, and is resolved toward the sacrifice (*entschlossen zum Tode*). With this trembling and this resolution, this book contributes to the realization of the ritual.

The large majority of the participants of the feast are not resolved in this way. On the contrary, they are resolved toward the continuation of the dance. From the perspective of this book, the large majority is precipitating itself toward small talk, toward repetitive nausea. But from the perspective of the majority, this precipitation is progress. From this perspective, this book's position is one that obstructs progress. Progress is, at this point of Western conversation, a ritual transformed into myth. From the perspective of the majority, this book's position is a sacrilegious position for obstructing a myth. Effectively, at this point of Western conversation, at the point where it comes closer to the confusion of languages, the large majority converses at a level of meaning that distances itself more and more from the level of meaning in this book. Western conversation is undoing itself in levels and layers, which makes the effort for the development of the conversation ever more painstaking. The large majority will only be able to think the thoughts contained in this book with a considerable effort of translation, just as this book also subjected itself to a considerable effort in order to translate the thoughts of the large majority to its own level. But this effort is part of the ritual of thought. It is precisely by disagreeing with the large majority that this book takes part in the ritual of the feast. The sacrifice that this book's position implies would only be valid if the vast majority took part in it. This book is, therefore, an effort toward an authentic conversation, because it intends to convert the vast majority. From this perspective we can already appreciate the precariousness of its position and the minimal hope it nurtures.

The sacrifice implies a radical modification of the character of Western conversation, since it modifies its aim. The intellect, no longer being an instrument of conquest, but of adoration, would no longer be the same intellect. The intellect, as we know it, would be sacrificed. It would be substituted by something currently unimaginable. The sacrifice would be an apocalyptic happening in the biblical sense of the phrase "they shall be changed." The sacrifice would imply a mutation in Western conversation. Facing this mutation, the attitude of this book is one of waiting. The doubt of doubt would be changed into something that can only very remotely be called "faith," because it would have nothing in common with the naive faith that preceded doubt in a remote phase of our feast. Therefore, the attitude of wait imposes itself. "They also serve, who only stand and wait."[2]

The great sources of our conversation, the initiators of our feast, the mythical figures of Orpheus and Abraham, of Ishtar and Aphrodite, these proper names so feted in explicatory rituals, call us in unison to the sacrifice, which they prefigure in their primordial vibration. We are in

---

2. Milton, John, Sonnet 16 ("On His Blindness"), 1652.

conversation with them, and not only with the Greeks, as Heidegger stated. Kierkegaard converses with Abraham in his supreme hour of sacrifice. It is through this type of conversation that the sacrifice could be realized. Let us hear the sources of our conversation, let us hear the proper names as they are whispered within us, and let us converse with those sources. Let us not blindly submit ourselves to them; let us doubt them. But let us not relegate them to oblivion, or wish to conquer and annihilate them. Let us continue the great adventure that thought is, but let us sacrifice the proud madness of wishing to dominate the all-different with our thought. Let us face the all-different by adoring it, that is, by being doubtful and submissive. In other words, let us once again be thinking beings; let us once again be humans.

Vilém Flusser (1920–1991) was born in Prague; emigrated to Brazil, where he taught philosophy and wrote a daily newspaper column; and later moved to France. Among his many books translated into English are *Language and Reality, Philosophy of Language,* and *Flusseriana,* all from Minnesota.

Rodrigo Maltez Novaes is a translator and research fellow at the Vilém Flusser Archive.

Siegfried Zielinski is professor of mediology and technoculture at the European Graduate School in Saas-Fee, Switzerland.